IN HER EYES

IN HER EYES
Reflections of a Father's Love

TOBY J. SWAGER

BRIA SWAGER

TATE PUBLISHING
AND ENTERPRISES, LLC

Published by Tate Publishing & Enterprises, LLC
127 E. Trade Center Terrace | Mustang, Oklahoma 73064 USA
1.888.361.9473 | www.tatepublishing.com

Tate Publishing is committed to excellence in the publishing industry. The company reflects the philosophy established by the founders, based on Psalm 68:11,
"The Lord gave the word and great was the company of those who published it."

Book design copyright © 2015 by Tate Publishing, LLC. All rights reserved.
Cover design by Joana Quilantang
Interior design by Gram Telen

Published in the United States of America

ISBN: 978-1-68142-105-6
1. Religion / Christian Life / Family
2. Religion / Christian Life / Relationships
15.03.26

Contents

Foreword

Hi! I'm Lexy Swager, and if you are like me, you love your dad unconditionally. If you are a parent and are like my dad, you love your kids so much you would do literally anything to make them happy. Now this doesn't mean I never get mad at him, but I can always be sure he is working to help me grow.

As we probably all know, fathers and daughters don't always see eye to eye. Sometimes that can result in a good thing that can help both grow. Sometimes it doesn't work out so well for either of them.

This does not mean that one of you is doing something wrong. It just means you have different opinions. You have to work on looking at the situation through the other person's eyes. This book will help you with that. Daughters, you get to see how what you say and how you act comes across to your dad. Fathers, you are being offered the opportunity to see how your actions and words look in her eyes.

Introduction

There is a common misconception in parenting today. We as fathers have encouraged it because of a desire to avoid uncomfortable conversation topics. The misconception is this: once a daughter reaches a particular age, she no longer needs strong paternal ties, but rather, she should turn to her mother for guidance and direction. Once the topics of breasts, boys, and menstrual cycles come to the forefront, dads often feel they have nothing to offer their little girl.

There are a number of reasons for this, and I, as a dad, understand to an extent the discomfort that comes from being a father to a budding young woman. But there is an inherent problem with the mind-set that says, "Since I'm a man, I couldn't possibly offer anything of value to the life of a little girl."

You see, we want them to always be just that, our little girl. We seem to think that we will be replaced as soon as there is a need for a bra, but that couldn't be farther from the truth. If anything, a daughter needs a strong paternal example in these formative years of her life. You have a great deal to offer even though you might not be able to relate directly to the issues at hand. After all, we as men have issues. We don't like to admit it, but we do. And though you might see those things we deal with as irrelevant to your daughter, they really aren't.

Now I'm not saying that we should bear all of our issues to our children. There needs to be restraint. What I am saying is simple: our issues should help us deal with (even if we don't understand) what our children are going through.

Typically, fathers begin to pull back from their daughters right at a time when girls struggle with confidence. Their bodies are changing, they are becoming young women. It's a difficult time for dads. We have to redefine our role. As soon as she begins to develop, she is no longer our little girl. We interact differently. We don't want to embarrass them or ourselves.

After all, when she was little, you didn't have to worry so much about where you touched her. She could run across the room and launch herself into the air, knowing beyond doubt that you would catch her. The only fear was where she landed, not how you caught her. Let's be honest. Most fathers wouldn't be comfortable if their fourteen-year-old daughter did the same thing. She has changed so much in such a short time, and we as dads don't feel comfortable with the changes, so it's just easier to avoid the situation all together.

I've had to have the talk with both my girls. No, not that talk, though I have been very much involved in those discussions as well. Let's just say I wasn't looking forward to sitting down over coffee and talking the birds and the bees, but it has to be done. What I mean is that I've talked with my daughters about the changes they are going through. I've let them know that there are a lot of things that Dad, even though I'm a pretty smart guy, isn't going to be able to give a definite answer about. For those things, they talk to their mom, or I talk to their mom and she handles it. But for the most part, I try to be very active in parenting my girls even through some things that aren't comfortable to talk about. They are natural parts of life that she shouldn't be embarrassed by, so neither should I.

I know this isn't the norm, but it should be. I believe there is a direct correlation between the changes a girl goes through during her tween years, how we respond to those changes, and the increase of societal problems like teen promiscuity, drug use, and pregnancy. As we change the way we relate to our daughters, it's only normal for a young woman to think something is wrong with her or to question if she is loved.

It's extremely important for a young woman to know that she is loved by her father. Her whole mind-set toward dating and adulthood is based on that knowledge. If, as a girl changes from child to adult, Dad begins to withdraw because he's not comfortable talking about things like boys and purses and makeup, it's only natural that she begin to feel rejected, even unloved. Those things that are happening to her at that moment are a very important part of her life, and though I don't enjoy shopping for woman's products or listening to my little girl talk about a boy being attractive, I have to because I'm her dad, and she needs me. It makes a huge impression on the life of your daughter to know that she has a father who loves her unconditionally. It's an investment that is guaranteed a high rate of return.

Bria

As a little girl, my dad was my knight in shining armor, my Prince Charming, my hero. Back then, it was easy to look up to my dad as my hero because it seemed there was always something we could do together. There was always some game to be played, or an adventure Barbie and her friends had yet to embark on, or a tickle fight to be fought. It was so easy, so simple, so natural.

Now that I'm older, it can be a bit harder to connect and a little more awkward. I mean, what teenage girl would be caught dead playing Barbie dolls at all, let alone with her dad? A teen girl isn't going to go around telling everyone she has a crush on her dad. She is much more likely to be focused on what her friends are doing, what she's going to wear, the new single from her favorite band, which boy from a said band is the cutest, or the next episode of that dumb television show than what her dad and she can do to spend time together. To tell the truth, the average teen is much more focused on what society thinks of them than what their parents think, and for a dad and his little girl, that tends to put a strain on the relationship.

Now instead of always wanting my dad around, there are a lot of times when I just want him to leave me alone and give me some space. I have often thought, *What does he know? He doesn't understand my situation.* Sometimes I'm right, he doesn't understand. But then, of course, I fail to realize that he can't possibly understand if I don't tell him what's going on.

Just because it's hard, doesn't mean we don't still get along and have moments. My dad is still my hero. He still encourages me and spends time with me. He is helping me become who God has called me to be. Because we still spend time together, my self-image has remained pretty positive. I'm not saying that I don't have times where I don't think that I'm pretty or that I'm fat, but it's a whole lot easier to handle times like that when I know that my dad still loves me. He hasn't stopped talking to me or spending time with me. We still hang out, even if it isn't always the same things we used to do. He still makes it a point, every chance he gets, to compliment me and tell me he loves me, which has made a lasting impression on what I see when I look in the mirror.

When I look at other girls who don't have their dad in their life like I do and just listen to what they say and how they act, I can't help but notice a difference. There is a direct correlation between the father-daughter relationship and a girl's confidence. When a girl's confidence is low, she can turn to things like boys, drugs, and sex to fill the gap left by her father. It is important that a dad doesn't just leave and try to pass everything off to Mom because the conversations can be awkward. Stay in your daughter's life throughout her tween and teen years. She will thank you, and you will thank yourself.

1

It's Nice to Be Needed!

The father-daughter relationship can be a confusing one. As a man, you feel completely inadequate and incapable of comprehending the complex changes your daughter goes through, both physically and emotionally, as she changes from your little girl to a young woman. And to be honest, you're right. We can't possibly understand what she is going through because it is a completely different process than what we encountered as young men at that age.

However, that doesn't mean we have nothing to offer at that stage of her life. It doesn't mean we should step away from the relationship while Mom comes in and takes it from here. We have the ability to empathize with our daughter. Because it seems so foreign to us, we often act as though nothing is changing, or that they've gone away for a little while, but we will be right here waiting for them when they return.

No matter how badly we may want to deny it, our daughters eventually will mature and become young women. One day, a young man will come by and sweep them off their feet. They will get married. They will be intimate with each other, and one day may even bless us with grandchildren. Awkward!

The fact of the matter is simple. We can't change it, so we need to accept it. All the more important that a firm foundation is established when she is young, which can be built upon during those times where communication can be strained between a dad and his little princess. In fact, that foundation is crucial to her self-image. Your communication with her now will help her make wise choices when those suitors present themselves. She won't be so susceptible to accept the advances of just any boy because she will have the self-confidence needed to not be swayed by the wooing words of a young man on the hunt. Your encouragement and love will help her to see through the phonies and find the one who is right for her, who will love her the way she deserves to be loved!

According to Jay Teachman, a professor of Sociology at Western Washington University, in an article from *The Journal of Family Issues* (January 2004), being raised by a single mother raises the risk of teen pregnancy, marrying with less than a high school degree, and forming a marriage where both partners have less than a high school degree. The website, www.growingupwithoutafather.org, reports, "In trying to satisfy their unmet emotional needs fatherless girls are more likely to be sexually promiscuous and are more vulnerable to the advances of predators who see their emotional needs and profit from them through commercial sex exploitation." It goes on to suggest that "official U.S. data shows that 63 percent of youth suicides (5 times the average), 70 percent of youths in state-operated institutions (9 times the average), and 85 percent of children with behavioral disorders (20 times the average) are from fatherless homes."

It even affects the physical development of girls. According to the site, "Women whose parents separated between birth and six years old experienced twice the risk of early menstruation," and they are "seven times more likely to get pregnant as an adolescent."

The statistics are extremely disturbing. They paint a bleak picture of a generation where the involvement of the father is nonexistent for a majority of adolescents. You have a huge role to play in the life of your child, whether boy or girl. Whether separated or parenting from a distance, the effects are the same. The positive impact of your time is a proven statistical fact!

As fathers, we need to take advantage of the time we have to mold them and teach them. A man's relationship with his daughters will establish a basis for a girl's self-image and self-confidence. We have a great responsibility, and it's more than just being the hero who comes to the rescue in the moment of need. It's being a shoulder she can cry on when she's hurting. A father should be a reassuring voice in the midst of all the chaos of daily life.

As she looks in the mirror, her reflection is greatly impacted not by what she sees, but by what you see! I get that it can be awkward as your daughter's body begins to change from child to young adult; in that moment, she needs you more than ever. No, I've never experienced the physical changes a girl goes through, but I can speak to the idea of change. I can't give advice on dealing with a menstrual cycle or picking out comfortable undergarments, but I must acknowledge the fact that she is changing.

It shouldn't be creepy or uncomfortable. When we can't talk honestly and openly about the processes of life, that's when those things become dirty, and when girls begin to doubt their self-worth. When a dad withdraws from showing affection to his daughter, she immediately begins to look in the mirror and wonder, "What's wrong with me?" She attributes the changes her body has gone through to her dad's distance. A foundation for shame begins to be built. She then looks for acceptance from other males who are more than willing to embrace the changes. Then begins a downward spiral of self-destructive behavior, motivated by a desire to fill the void left from the change in the father-daughter relationship.

I don't want to overly simplify this point! I believe a girl's image reflects the affection her father has shown her. If Dad establishes a healthy, positive image based on the whole person—inside and out—building character, as well as confidence in the person she is and will be, the chance of that young lady seeking her identity in other sources is slim to nonexistent. She needs to know she is worthy of love just because she is worthy, not because of what she can do or what she can offer someone! And that comes from a dad who establishes a healthy, loving relationship with that young woman.

Hug her when she's hurting. Hold her hand and sing silly songs with her! Take her to a movie and teach her that she is precious and deserves to be respected by that young man who will come knocking all too soon. The topic of sex and boys needs to be discussed by Dad, as well as Mom, and not just from the "cleaning my gun" approach. As we joke about those things, they seek answers from other sources.

If we aren't doing everything we should to properly arm our children with the knowledge they need for the world they *will* face, what right do we have to criticize when they make decisions with which we disagree? We should be their source, regardless of the discomfort the topic may present us. The world is more than willing to fill the void we leave if we choose to allow the discomfort to determine our course of action!

So sit down with her. Tell her that she's more than a pretty face, that her value comes from within. Build her up so that the things she will encounter in life don't tear her down. She needs you to combat the hurtful words of other young men and women going through the same changes but who don't have the positive source in their lives, encouraging them and building their self-image. Without it, she could easily be swayed to change her look, her behavior, or even who she is, in order to find acceptance. Girls with a strong foundation don't need acceptance from their peers because they know their value doesn't hinge on the words of a few, but it comes from inside and doesn't have anything to do with how they look, how they walk, or what they wear.

Like I said, it's a huge responsibility. You're going to make mistakes. You'll look at her wrong and make her cry, or you'll say something and discover now is not a good time to say *anything*, let alone something like that. Don't allow fear of failing to keep you from being involved in her life. Those hurts are temporary, but the hurt caused by doubting her self-worth can be lifelong. She will question whether she is lovable at some point in her life. Make sure you've undoubtedly answered that question.

Bria

A girl needs her father just as much as she needs her mother. She needs her dad to show her love so that she doesn't go looking for it in the wrong places. A girl needs her dad to be there for her when she is little, not just at work all the time. Don't get me wrong; a father should support his family, but he has to make time to spend with his family as well. By spending time with his daughter when she is young, he creates a firm foundation for when she is older.

Without a firm foundation, the relationship is not likely to stand through the trials of the teen years.

During puberty, a girl goes through a lot of changes that can be scary for both a girl and her dad. It is all too normal for a dad to step aside and let Mom handle it. A girl needs her dad through this time to show her that he still supports her. When her dad is always there, she feels more confident in who she is, even as a little girl. If that constant support from a male role model is taken away too soon, a girl can lose faith in herself easily. So don't stop being the knight in shining armor just because your little girl is growing up. Stay beside her and help her as much as you can, and consult Mom when you are completely lost.

As a father, you have more responsibilities when it comes to your daughter's relationships than critiquing the boys and scaring them half to death. Every child, boy or girl, needs an example of what love is. The first place they get it is in their parents. Don't set a bad example for your children. Also, as a father, you need to always show your daughter what to expect from a young man. If she does not get a good example from you and her mother, she will turn to other things to show her what love is, like television and movies. These are not the best examples for any child, girl or boy. So make sure they get a good example from you and will not rely so much on media to tell them what love is.

I have previously stated that a girl needs her daddy when she is little to be more than just a provider. I can promise you, there is not some crazy hormone that switches that off when a girl turns thirteen. A girl needs her daddy during the teen years just as much as when she is little, sometimes more so. Don't back out of your daughter's life just because she has started puberty, or even if she says she wants you to. She needs you, whether she realizes it or not.

If you are building something, you have to make a firm foundation first if you want the structure to last. However, if you don't build on that foundation, all you have is a platform of stone in the ground. It is the same with the father-daughter relationship. A firm foundation when a child is young is important, but you have to build on that foundation during the teen years to make the relationship really meaningful and beautiful.

A teenage girl needs her father as much as she did when she was a sweet little kid playing with Barbies. She needs someone to come alongside her and protect her. The relationship between a father and daughter can be a beautiful thing. Just make sure you don't focus entirely on the foundation and forget about the rest.

2

Dad Isn't Just a Name

If we think a title, like *boss* or *dad*, requires that we be respected, we're only fooling ourselves. We cannot demand respect because of who we are. Respect is earned. Respect demanded is fueled by fear, and it's ineffective. It isn't real respect. People can only operate in fear for so long before they fight against what they fear, or they run from it. Demanding respect is as effective as demanding rain from a clear sky. It won't happen. True respect comes from loving those we lead.

When people realize that you are willing to set aside yourself for them, laying down your life, your desires, so they can have what they need more than anything—your time—you build a foundation that's solid. That foundation helps bring the respect we long for, not because of who we are, but because of what we will do for those we lead!

You can't beat a child to respect you! You can lead them through love, guiding them because they recognize you are willing to do whatever you ask them to do. Too many people abuse the title that gives them the power to tell people what to do; that isn't real power! Real power comes from real love. Real love builds respect, and respect should be mutual. If it isn't, it's being demanded and is motivated by fear of punishment.

Now punishment is necessary, but it shouldn't be used to force respect. It is the end result of what we sow. If the motivation behind the punishment is to require respect from the person being punished, it won't work. We will cause the person, whether it's our child or someone else we're leading, to build resentment and destroy any genuine respect that person felt for us.

If we respect our kids, then we should love them enough to lead them. Our love and respect for them will foster mutual respect. Respect can't be demanded, and it can't be faked! People can see through fake actions easily, and you can only manipulate people for a short time before they feel frustration and resentment. We devalue those from whom we demand respect whether through falseness or fear. When we devalue someone, we disrespect them. How unreasonable is it for us to expect respect from those we don't value, just because of our position in life. There's a word for that: tyranny.

Tyrants demand love and respect out of fear. Eventually, people will fight to come out of the grip of any tyrant. They recognize that the one demanding respect is self-serving and seeking to get what they can out of those they are using. It doesn't work. Throughout history, it has never worked. It doesn't work when leading a nation, and it certainly won't work when leading a family.

Our families need to know beyond a doubt that we love them and will lay down our lives for them. If you want respect in your home, give respect. The Golden Rule may seem a little antiquated, but it's as effective today as when it was first penned. The easiest way to get respect is to give it. Love those whom you are leading, and they will be willing to lay down their lives for you. We should be willing to do anything we require of those we lead, even giving up our own life.

Real respect builds relationships faster than anything other than love! Love is essential for real respect. We can't respect what we don't love. Respect fosters trust! Trust is necessary for respect to grow and for healthy relationships to become even stronger!

It takes work to raise a family. It's incredibly hard but extremely rewarding. The time spent building your relationships within your family will reap a huge harvest in time. I think the hardest part is finding the balance between all of life's demands. We typically have children at a time in our lives when we are building our futures and our careers. We often sacrifice one for the other, expecting understanding. We often don't see what's lost until it's too late to do anything about it. If we want to foster real relationships and genuine respect, we need to invest the time and strive to make our kids see that we value them.

Every minute invested in your child is worth far more than any pay you will receive from your job. Each minute you set aside for them strengthens the bond between parent and child and fosters respect, because you aren't putting everything else before them. Work is necessary, but it doesn't speak love to a child who can't understand why Dad or Mom isn't there to hear them speak at their preschool graduation. There will be times when life requires you to miss an occasional concert or game, but you should never miss more than you attend. That's not balance. It doesn't bring respect.

Most kids look at Mom and Dad as their funding source because we often put work ahead of teaching them the value of a dollar. We allow the guilt of not being there to push us to buy their affection. We may get a temporary burst of appreciation, but we can never buy the respect of our kids. They need to see that we are willing to go without certain things because spending time teaching them, walking through this life with them, is more important than having things. Those things we want eventually consume us and take even more time away. Respect requires time. Without it, your relationship will be strained. Mutual respect leads to great relationships between a parent and a child. It's worth it. No matter what it takes, foster a relationship built on love and respect between you and your kids. It will last through any storm life throws your way.

Bria

Respect is an important aspect of any relationship. It comes into play in some capacity for every person in a relationship, no matter what type of relationship. Without respect, there really would never be any good points in a relationship.

A simple example would be knocking on a door before entering a room and waiting for an answer. If I am in my room, or any room, and the door is closed, I would like whoever wishes to enter to knock before they do so. Also, after they knock, to wait for an answer. Is it too much to ask that someone knock and wait a moment after doing so, so I can respond? Knocking on a door before entering one is a common courtesy and should be respected in any relationship.

There are many common courtesies that should go without saying, like knocking on a door before entering or asking to borrow something, instead of assuming that it is okay to take it. However, there are other things that sometimes have to be said aloud for some reason; things like not talking back to one's parents or other authority figures, taking headphones out of the ears when talking to someone, or looking at someone when talking to them. Occasionally, these things have to be said, even if it seems that they should be common sense.

There are other things, still, that have to be said. A silly example would be not talking or texting during a movie at a theater, or while someone is doing some sort of school work in the same room. Different things annoy different people, and many times it can be seen as disrespectful to say something to one person, while it is perfectly alright to say the same thing to someone else.

Being respectful can be confusing. Some people turn to the Golden Rule and say, "Treat others as you want to be treated." However, I have found that this is not always true. For example, I may want someone to tell me something straightforward without watering it down, so I may go to someone and ask them to, and they may take offense. Most of the time, the Golden Rule works; however, just keep in mind that there are always exceptions to the rule, just like any rule in the English language.

It is commonly accepted that a child should respect his or her parents, and I am by no means saying that they should not respect their parents; quite the opposite, actually. Children and teens should respect their parents and other authority figures, even if they don't agree with them. A child or teen should listen to their parents and respect them. I am not saying that I do this perfectly because if I do, I would be lying. I do not always respect my parents the way that I should, and I am working on it. However, the real problem comes when a child completely disrespects their parents on purpose, and sometimes this may stem from a feeling that either their parents haven't earned their respect, or they do not feel respected, or both.

It is not only the child who should respect the parents. There is an amount of respect that should come from the parent. Respect has to be earned, but don't hold out on your kids. Respect is not just a lesson for kids to learn, but one for adults as well. Respect their privacy and their decisions. The second one especially comes into play with teenagers. There comes a time when you, as a parent, are going to have to trust that you have taught your child well and respect their decisions. For example, if you have a kid who you want to play soccer, but they decide that they want to do theater instead, you should be able to love and respect them enough to respect their decision.

Respect is important in every relationship, the parent-child relationship included. Respect should come from both sides of a relationship. The child is not the only one who should show respect, but the parent should show their child respect as well. So remember, expect respect from your kids, but don't forget to give it to them when they earn it.

3

Perception versus Reality

For a long time, I struggled in my relationship with my daughters. I assumed people saw me as lazy because a small number of people hinted to that notion. Their opinions pushed me to question what I was doing, and whether or not I was hurting my kids. Even though their perception was not our reality, I allowed it to affect me in ways that were very unhealthy. I knew I was doing what was right for our family, but I was so concerned with the opinions of others that I began to change what we were doing in a vain attempt to gain their approval.

Eventually, I got past that need for everyone to accept how my wife and I had decided to raise our kids. Our girls have faired well. Better than well actually. They are both exceptionally smart, great students and excellent friends to those around them. They have incredible hearts for the hurting and truly love people no matter what they have done. I might be a little biased, but I think our kids are great, and given the opportunity, they will change the world around them for the better.

Perception is a strange force in our lives. It can cause our reality to become distorted. We believe things that aren't true, based on how we perceive the world around us. For example, a person assumes that a kindness shown to them by a person of the opposite sex is actually something more. They pursue the feelings that they perceive to exist because they misinterpreted an act of kindness as an act of love. Many a broken heart has had it's beginnings in misperception. It's how most stalkers get their start!

It may seem a little extreme, but it's fact. Our perception can cause us to make rash decisions about a person because we misinterpreted something that was said or done. That's why I'm such a huge fan of the American-Indian proverb: "Never judge a man until you've walked a mile in his moccasins." It's a great way to avoid misinterpretation and hurt feelings. It also helps you to better understand why, from their perspective, your path might not be the right one.

Ultimately, each man or woman's path is their own, and it's not for me to determine where they made a wrong turn. Even for my kids, I can have an opinion of what they need to do, and it might be a well-educated position that I am coming from, but perhaps my goal for their life isn't exactly the same direction they feel led to go. It doesn't make me wrong for hoping great things for their lives. What would be wrong would be to force them to go the direction I perceive to be right, regardless of what they believe to be right for them. I need to support them, not demand that they become who I hoped they would be. My perception might be wrong because the lens I'm looking through might not match the lens they need to achieve what their life holds for them.

Even the most evil among us believe themselves to be in the right. There is a line in one of my family's favorite movie that speaks to this very fact: "You're going to find that many of the truths we hold to are based solely upon our point of view." Obi Wan was right; the people we encounter, who try to change our path because they perceive we are going the wrong way are basing their opinion on their own point of view. We can't possibly see things clearly if we refuse to look from the perspective of those we are trying to help. We have to be able to understand that their advice isn't meant to hurt us, they simply don't have all the facts because they aren't standing in your shoes.

Perception is tricky. Sometimes it's right on, and other times it's 180 degrees from fact, but we believe it because it's how we see things from our point of view. Perception can pull us so far from reality that we will decide to do what's wrong and believe that it's right. Even Hitler thought he was right, and his passion for what he believed led many others astray.

When we allow the perception of others to dictate our reality, we find ourselves drifting from the plan that God has for us. Hold onto what you know to be right for you.

Don't jump to conclusions based on your perception of the facts. As a dad, you have a responsibility to teach your children in the way they should go. Don't allow a fear that your actions will be perceived incorrectly stop you from being the dad that you need to be.

I remember being worried about holding my daughter's hand in public because people might get the wrong idea. How ridiculous is that? She might be nearing adulthood, but she still needs to know that her daddy loves her. Just because society has made things awkward doesn't mean we shouldn't be who we're meant to be for our kids. Our girls need fathers who love them unconditionally.

Perception affects the way we parent in so many ways. From the way our kids perceive us as parents to the way our parents, friends, and coworkers see us, it can be very easy to lose sight of the plan for our own lives. If we are blown about by the perceptions of others, we put our relationship with our kids at risk. The opinions of those around shouldn't dictate the way we raise our children. The direction of your life isn't the same as theirs. Try walking in each others moccasins for a while; it will shed light on the choices of the people around you every day. It's much easier to love and appreciate people when you try to see things from their point of view. In the end, that's what really matters. Love people, love God and let that love change the world.

Bria

Perception is a huge part of life. Villains and heroes are based on our perception of the world. In practically every story, the character who is labeled as the villain thinks that they are in the right, even though the people around them don't see it the same way. In many of my favorite shows and movies, the villain who has decided to wipe out the entire human race thinks that he is right in doing so. He thinks that he is better than humanity and that humans are corrupt and evil, so, naturally, they need to be wiped out. I am not saying that I take the villain's side in many stories, but I can empathize with them.

One of the best examples I can think of is the evil stepmother in the story, Cinderella. We all know the story. Cinderella's father gets married and dies, leaving little Cinderella in the care of her stepmother. Now, just for a moment, I want you to forget everything you know about that particular story. Imagine it from the stepmother's perspective.

Her first husband is gone, leaving her with two daughters to support. Now she finds a new husband to take care of her, and she thinks that everything is finally going to work out. But then, just shortly after they were married, he dies. It would be completely natural for her to become bitter. Then she thinks back and realizes that her late husband loved his daughter Cinderella more than her daughters, or even herself. In her anger, she blames Cinderella and makes her do all the chores. She reduces the person who, in her mind, kept her husband from truly loving her daughters and herself. She wants the best for her daughters, so when she hears that there is a ball at which the prince will choose his bride, she sees the perfect opportunity to give her daughters what she always wanted for them. Then the issue of Cinderella comes to mind. I have to think about what went through her head. She had to think back of the love that her late husband showed Cinderella, which she felt her own daughters deserved. She had to think that if her own husband loved Cinderella over herself and her daughters, how could the prince choose one of her daughters over Cinderella? So she does everything she can to keep Cinderella from the ball. Toward the end, she even goes so far as to break the glass slipper to try to stop Cinderella from getting what she feels her daughters deserve.

Now that you have a different perspective on the story, think about how the stepmother saw herself and compare it to how everyone else saw her. In the stepmother's mind, she was doing the right thing. She was trying to get the best life she could for her daughters. She ignored the fact that her tactics hurt others. In the eyes of others, however, she was evil. She treated her stepdaughter like garbage. She didn't care who she knocked down in her quest for power.

This is a common issue in real people. People forget to take into account the different points of view that are in the world. We go about our business, many times thinking that we are doing everything right and that no one has any reason to be angry with us. Then we are shocked when someone gets angry at us for something that seemed so benign to us.

This dynamic comes into play in every relationship, and sometimes it works the opposite way than people commonly think it does. Many times, people think that other people hate them when, in truth, they don't have anything against them. It can be very difficult to balance perception and reality, but it is vital to human life if we are to be effective in this world.

4

Oh, to Be a Knight!

When our daughters are younger, it's so much simpler. They are easier to understand and easier to satisfy. A few moments spent playing with dolls, with her styling your hair, or making a craft builds valuable memories that will last for a lifetime. You become the hero in their eyes when you stop and take even a small amount of time.

We are the heroes! We can tickle away the tears, and our kiss heals the most trivial of boo-boos. We are supercool and can do anything in their eyes. We dance with them at an imaginary ball and laugh with them, as their favorite cartoon character does something absolutely ridiculous. I remember so many times when my daughters and I would laugh at the silliest things—laugh until our stomachs hurt. I remember crying with them when they were hurting and celebrating the victories they achieved.

From the first moments I held each one, they had my heart. I determined to make a difference in each of their lives no matter what I had to set aside. Typically, it costs me nothing more than a few dollars and my pride, but it's been worth the investment. Pride isn't that great, and money, though nice to have, doesn't last for long with three ladies in the house (especially when your wife loves shoes).

You see, I decided that having daughters who knew they were loved was worth the embarrassing pictures of me with barrettes in my hair. I was making a deposit for the long-term in an account that can't come back empty. Being silly with your children doesn't make them disrespect you, it has the opposite effect. When we are willing to get down on their level, it speaks something to a child.

Playing with dolls can be a little awkward, and going to see the latest, greatest singer in 3-D, or a musical on ice isn't something you'll see me doing often, but it's one of my favorite activities when my girls are involved. Seeing their smiles when the basketball star from a certain musical that shall go unnamed, lands a triple salchow after shooting the game-winning shot (it's gotta be hard to play basketball on ice skates) makes it worth the ribbing you get from your friends. It takes a real man to sit through some of those things (Justin Bieber in 3-D comes to mind).

Those moments built a firm foundation. Though we don't always see eye to eye, we have a relationship that isn't destroyed by disagreement. In fact, there are really few things we disagree about. We have an honest relationship. My daughters know they can ask me anything, and they also know they shouldn't ask me something they don't want answered honestly.

We talk about things that most dads feel uneasy discussing. Communication is essential. I may have a slight advantage from my years as a youth pastor, but it's still awkward talking with them about topics like boys, puberty, and sex. After all, these are my kids. I want them to be proud of their dad, not embarrassed by me (okay, sometimes I want them to be embarrassed, but not always). Oftentimes, the hardest things for us are even harder for our kids. They want to ask the questions, but they don't know how we will respond, or they think we will get upset by what they've asked.

Being a knight would be so much easier. You would chase after the fair maiden in distress. You would battle the most atrocious of foes to win the hand of the lady or the princess. You would be willing to die to protect the honor of the woman who holds your heart. As a dad, you didn't have to worry about as much, or you were a little more naive. Young men had honor, and every little girl wanted to be the recipient of love's true kiss.

Fighting for their honor and their love is so much harder now. We have so many more things competing for their affection, and honor seems to be a thing of the past! That's why it's even more important to instill those values and ideals in their heart while you have the chance. They will seek out their knight in shining armor if we will be the example they need us to be!

Bria

Every girl, little or big, dreams of meeting a knight in shining armor. The only problem with this is that in our society, girls seem to forget what being a knight means. Some girls forget to look past the handsome face and big muscles to see what it really means to be a knight. King Arthur's knights of the Round Table did not achieve the title of knight on looks and charm alone. Knights were chivalrous. They had to have six things to even be considered for knighthood: fairness, nobility, valor, honor, courtesy, and loyalty. They would never attack an unarmed foe, cheat, or abandon a friend. They were to always exhibit self discipline, protect the innocent, show courage, keep their word, be polite, and respect women.

Many young men in today's world have sadly forgotten the Code of Chivalry, as have many young women. Many girls forget what it means to be truly respected during their teen years. They don't hold very high standards for young men anymore; otherwise, there would not be so many teen pregnancies today. They mistake attention for love and respect, and that leads to heartbreak. A lot of heartbreak could be avoided if girls held boys, and boys held themselves, to the standards of the Code of Chivalry. Sadly, the standards of today's world are not as high as they used to be, and that is where a father comes in to the equation.

As a father, it is your responsibility to give your daughter an example of true love and respect from an early age. Make sure she knows what to expect from a young man. Be a knight for her, and not just when she is a little girl. When she is a teenager, continue to show her love and respect. You have to make sure she understands how valuable she is because she will go looking for value in other places that will lead to heartbreak, places that she never should have had to look in the first place.

If you show her what it is to be a knight, then she will know what to look for in a young man. This means that you need to be a knight all the time, not just when you are talking directly to her. Show her true love and respect through your relationship with her mother and everyone else in your life. It is easier to be a knight when you are doing it all day everyday instead of just when you are with her.

Also, by becoming a knight yourself, you will be able to lead others by example. You may influence the young men around you, which would lead to a chain reaction. You becoming a knight could change not just your daughter's expectations for young men, but it could change others' as well. One of the main reasons chivalry has passed out of the norm is because fathers let it pass. Many young men do not even know how to be a knight because there is no one in their life to show them what it means to be chivalrous.

So be the hero. Be the knight in shining armor. Live by the Code of Chivalry. Living a life of honor will lead others to do the same. When you show your princess what she should expect from a knight in shining armor, you will spare her an enormous amount of heartbreak. She will have higher standards, and these standards will aid her in not becoming another sad statistic because she will not settle for anything less than a true knight.

5

One Day, Her Prince Will Come

I do realize, much to my chagrin, that some day a young man will come to our door, asking to see our daughter. After I make silly jokes about seeing with the eyes and not the hands, I will be left to trust that the values I have instilled in her will be stronger than the advances of a said young man. Hopefully, she will choose her beau wisely, using prayerful consideration so that Daddy isn't forced into the awkward position of explaining why the poor boy wet his pants after dropping her off.

I don't take lightly the responsibility I have to teach my daughters what a gentleman looks like and how he should behave. I have tried to exemplify the character of a gentleman when I take them on daddy-daughter dates, or when they see their mother and me interacting in both the public eye and at home. I'm not perfect, and I have made many mistakes. But it's the ability to recognize those mistakes and correct them that sets apart a true gentleman.

It leaves an impression of what to seek out when they are looking for that special guy. I am not suggesting that they should or will marry miniature versions of myself. By all means, the young man will have his own upbringing and character to add to the equation, but I am trying to establish a benchmark in key areas that point to motivation for behaviors.

Trust me, I pity the young man who comes into our home, trying to win my hand instead of my daughters'. I will see through the smoke screen he is setting quicker than politicians change their stand! If he is more interested in me liking him, then chances are he's hoping to hide his real interest in my daughter through flattery. He will be doomed. My daughters will see that boy coming a mile away.

I'm not looking for perfection. I understand people will make mistakes, but these are my daughters. Let's limit the mistakes to things outside the relationship. It really would be in everyone's best interest!

The young man should be confident in who he is and love God with all his heart. He must understand, without my explaining to him, the value of his relationship with God comes ahead of his relationship with my daughter. He should be respectful of her and willing to play by our rules. Anyone who isn't probably won't be in the running for long.

What can I say? I set the mark pretty high for a reason. My daughters deserve a young man who will cherish them for who they are, inside and out. They aren't arm candy. They are intelligent, loving people who put others ahead of themselves. They should be encouraged to chase their dreams and fulfill there goals.

I know, eventually, that day will come. I secretly hope for joy and fulfillment in their lives from the man God intends for my girls. I'm not naive. I know what the world is like and what people are like. My hope is that I have shared quality moments with each of my daughters that will inspire them to not settle, but seek that one young man intended to complete them.

It may seem like an overly romantic ideal, but it it's not. When they say, "I do" or "I will," I want it to be for the right reasons, and with the understanding that this is something to be worked on for a lifetime. It will only last if the commitment supersedes the attraction. Relationships are hard but worth every minute of struggle. Attraction is easy and often leads us to places we don't want to go, making choices we don't want to make.

I hope, for my girls' sake, they are praying for that boy even now. Without God, it's nearly impossible to stay committed in this world. And I hope that his parents are praying for my girls because they aren't exactly perfect either, but they are close.

Bria

I am honestly terrified of the day a boy asks me out. I know that someday my prince will come; but I'm not entirely sure how I will respond to him, or how I will tell my dad. I mean, am I just supposed to come home and tell my dad, "Hey, a boy asked me out today."? Do I tell my mom, then have her tell my dad? I really don't know what I will do.

Most of the time, this is a subject I discuss with my mom. We will have random talks in the grocery store or while we are out on a walk. Sometimes I'll start the conversation by asking some question like "What do I do when a boy asks me out?" or "When will I be able to go on dates?" Most girls know not to ask their dad questions such as these; with their mom, they can expect a serious answer. Dad, however, usually gives an answer like thirty-five, sixty-seven, or never. Anyway, usually these conversations consist of my mom and me talking about the few boys my age that I think are "boyfriend material." She understands that while I may think someone is cute doesn't necessarily mean I will date them. This is the case with most girls. But dads, don't let this discourage you from talking to your little girl about boys. Don't smother her; let mom take the lead some of the time, but don't completely back out of this issue. Girls still need their daddy, even if they think that they don't.

Now, as I previously stated, I don't normally talk to my dad about these kinds of things; however, they do come up occasionally. He will ask something like, "So how many boys asked you out today?" And I will respond with, "None, Daddy." Then he acts like he doesn't believe me. He also likes to entertain guests with his plots and schemes for the boy who comes to pick me up for a date, especially when I am present. The stories range from wearing bubba teeth to showing off his gun collection to handing the poor boy a dummy grenade, after pulling the pin and saying, "Hold on to this for a minute. I'll go get Bria." I'm not sure who I feel sorrier for: me or the guy.

Dads, do not assume that your only job in your daughter's love life is to be the "bad guy" and scare the boy off. It is your job to make sure that a boy is good enough for your little princess, and she may not always appreciate it at first, but one day she will realize that you love her and that is why you do what you do.

Another responsibility you have is to set an example for your daughter and show her what to expect from a young man. An excellent way to do this is to take her on daddy-daughter dates and not just while she is little. Take your little girl on at least one date a year throughout her tween and teen years. If you have more than one daughter, one date with both (or all) of them together is great; however, occasionally you should take each girl on a date. Daddy-daughter dates were defining moments in my childhood and my relationship with my dad. My dad has often taken both my little sister and me together on one date, and those were fun. However, sometimes I just needed time for just me and Daddy, and so did Lexy. It doesn't have to be anything extravagant. Just make sure it is something that interests her. My dad has it easy: since he was a stay-at-home-dad, he rubbed off on Lexy and me quite a bit, so he ended up with two girls who love superhero movies and sports games. However, as I said before, it can be as simple as dinner and a movie, or just dinner, or dinner and shopping afterward. Just make sure it is something both of you will enjoy.

The good thing for me is I know what to expect from a boy. My dad has been showing me that for as long as I can remember. I know that he needs to respect me, and I know that my dad will protect me, even if it is embarrassing for me. I know what a man of God looks like because I have seen it in my dad. I know that God has a plan for my life, and someday, there will be a man who sweeps me off my feet, and I will have my "happily ever after" moment.

6

Daddy-Daughter Dating

I'll never forget the moments I've spent molding my daughters' expectations from the boy who will someday come calling. We've made so many memories along the way, but our daddy-daughter dates are some of my favorites. It doesn't have to be fancy, though it is fun to dress up on occasion. In fact, I've even taken them hunting and fishing. Might not sound like much of a date to you, but the opportunities to talk about life are endless when you're sitting on a dock, waiting for a fish to tug the line.

When I think about all the dates we've had, from individual time spent with one daughter or the other to the times I've taken them both out with me, there is one or two that standout as my favorites. There was the time I took both my daughters to a fancy Japanese steak house where they cook in front of you, and then to the daddy-daughter Valentine's dance at our local community center. Both my girls got all dressed up and looked like princesses, and we danced and laughed all night long. It was so refreshing to see so many other fathers investing in their daughter's lives.

It says a lot to a girl when Dad will dress in his best and dance around with them to their favorite songs. It teaches them to value themselves for who they are, not for what they have to offer someone.

There was the time I took my oldest to see Monsters, Inc. after her baby sister was born. I wanted her to know that even though there was a great deal of attention going to our new addition, she was still as important as ever. It was so much fun watching the movie and then going to every McDonald's for miles around to find all of the "Happy Meal" toys that came out with the movie. I remember being so frustrated, probably more than her, when on our date, she didn't get a toy in her "Happy Meal."

Every dad should take time to pour into his daughter and, for a moment, make her feel like she is the most important person in the room. Give her the attention she craves because if you don't, she will look for it elsewhere. And don't let cost stand in the way either. The value comes from the time you invest, not the money that you spend. We feel inadequate so we cover our own insecurities with money, but all she really wants is your ear and your time.

It can be a walk at the park and a picnic where she tells you her dreams, and you dare to dream with her, encouraging her to become everything she hopes. We can crush them all too easily when we talk down to them because their dreams seem too big to us. That little time spent encouraging could be the difference between believing in herself and struggling to find an identity, seeking acceptance in all the wrong ways.

We so often make the mistake of thinking that if I had money, I'd do so much more. It holds us back from establishing the kind of relationship that we should with our kids. We think money replaces time spent, but an extra fifty dollars a week can't replace the four hours it took to earn it. We get so much more return on time invested with our kids than money spent. I know we live in a world that seems controlled by the almighty dollar. We've made it this way. We have to get back to finding value in the small moments, taking each day as a new opportunity to make an impact in our children's lives.

You should plan an occasional time where you spoil them with a fancy dinner, but when that is the norm it becomes expected. It needs to be special. So much more can come of a simple time spent talking, sharing, and encouraging. Go to the park and play on the swings together! Laugh together; be silly and ridiculous. Allow yourself to relax! You won't lose their respect from a moment of silliness. Your willingness to come to their level will only solidify their belief that you love them.

Let them talk about faraway places and castles and all those things that little girls dream about! Be their prince as they act out their favorite fairytale! It makes all the difference to the little girl who wants to be loved and needs to believe that she's worth fighting for. Establish that belief at an early age, and she will be more prepared for the things she will face later in life!

And don't let age stop you from taking advantage of the moments you are given to teach and mold your daughter. Whether she is six or sixteen, she still needs to know she is your princess! It isn't awkward, at least it shouldn't be. If it is, something has happened along the way to make it awkward. Our responsibility as dad doesn't stop because they are older. It's necessary that we make an effort, regardless of age.

She needs you to love her mother and set an example of what a loving husband will do for his wife. Complement her and mean it, for no other reason than she is the love of your life. Show your daughter that you're still willing to fight and lay down your life for her mother, after all the time you've been together. Don't be afraid to show affection (within reason) in front of your kids! They need to see you holding your wife's hand and kissing her from time to time. You are the example whom they will follow! If you don't give them an example, then they will turn to anything or anyone who will.

You're molding your daughter's ideal of a man, and she will pursue it, whether you mold something good or something bad! Most young ladies find themselves in relationships later in life that reflect the relationship they saw modeled in the home. That includes abusive relationships as well as healthy ones.

Don't overlook the importance of spending the time necessary to make a lasting impression that your little girl will hold onto, long after your time dressing up for playdates is over! Your relationship is the foundation for every relationship they will have as adults. Make it count! Love her mother and love your little girl so that one day, she will find a true prince of a young man, and all her dreams will come true!

There are so many potential date ideas. Don't feel like you have to be stuck to the typical dinner and a movie! We've gone to sporting events (fortunately, my daughters enjoy them, or at least they say they do; maybe it's just the time we spend together at them), dances, banquets, movies (of course), school functions, even one of those "On Ice" shows where their favorite movies at the time were presented in a dazzling spectacle filled with spins and songs galore! It seemed pretty hard for the guys to play basketball on ice, but they didn't have any trouble singing "Get in The Game" while skating around the rink.

Sure it's not always my favorite thing, and it shouldn't be. The point is to establish a foundation for what they will expect from that young man who comes calling someday. Your daughter should be confident enough to express her desires, from restaurants she likes to activities they enjoy together. Any boy worth her time certainly should consider what she wants to do, even if it is watching a bunch of people reenact all three High School Musicals on ice. He better be willing to sing the songs with her. If not, she will have the confidence to know that he isn't the one and move on. She doesn't need to be a victim just so he will like her.

That's what we do as fathers. We establish a baseline, and she will look back throughout her life and compare her relationships with your relationship with her mother. She will expect young men to treat her the same way you treated her when she was younger. She will most likely receive love through a language she learned watching you. If you buy her lots of gifts, she's going to expect it from that young man. If you give her your time, that's what she will want in a husband one day. Don't underestimate your impact, and don't overlook the opportunities you have to impress good quality and values in her heart and mind. She will thank you for it one day!

Bria

Some of my fondest memories are of dates that I have with my dad. We have done a vast array of activities to spend time together, from fishing to car shows to movies to dinners and dances. They all showed me how much my dad loves me, as much now as before.

One specific time, we went to a daddy-daughter dance at a local community center. It was a lot of fun. Lexy and I were wearing pretty dresses, and my dad was dressed up slightly. We danced and sang and even entered the father-daughter look-alike contest. It was just a fun night of twirling and laughing with my dad that showed me that I was loved truly by my daddy.

My first daddy-daughter date, though I don't remember it much, was to go see Monsters, Inc. This particular date was just between me and my dad, and it explains my love for a big fluffy blue-and-purple "kitty" and his little green one-eyed friend. I have always loved this movie. While it is a good heart-warming movie, I can't help but realize that my adoration of this particular animated feature has something to do with the fact that the first time I saw it was during my first daddy-daughter date. Whether it be a story of two monsters trying to get a little girl back home safe, a boy band's concert made into a movie, or a ragtag group of losers trying to save the galaxy, or even something as simple as taking me to see a great movie, shows me how much my dad loves me.

The most recent date my dad and I have been on was a rather unorthodox one. My sister was going to a friend's birthday party on this particular day, so when I saw a sign at our local park about a car show, I suggested to my dad that we go there and then to lunch at a restaurant to which I had recently won a gift card. My dad liked the idea, but it turned out that the youth pastor at our church was moving that same day, and he desperately needed some help. So, in the morning of our date, my dad proposed that we go to the car show for a little while, then go help our pastor move, and then eat lunch. I was fine with this idea. I had helped my dad move people before, and I didn't mind. We got there, and there was no one there to help. So we got started. I helped move a few boxes and things, but the whole time their young son was underfoot, wanting to help. So to make a long story short, I ended up watching the son while they moved stuff. We were there until about four in the afternoon, which was not what we expected. We took a quick trip to Walmart, got my dad a shirt to change, and then went to get an appetizer so we would have some room for dinner.

Now while you may be thinking that this was a horrible experience, and that you feel sorry for me, I would tell you that you are wrong. I was glad to help out in any way I could, even if that ended up being keeping a four-year-old out of the way for a few hours. The whole time, my dad kept apologizing and saying that I should just tell him when I wanted to leave, but I, being so much like him, kept reassuring him that it was fine. We stayed until they got the truck packed. I truly didn't mind helping people on our date. That experience just made the experience all the more memorable. It will be very hard for me to forget that day, and not only did my dad and I create a few memories together, but we blessed a family at the same time.

It doesn't take much to show your daughter that you love her. It doesn't have to be anything expensive. Now occasionally, a nicer dinner might be in order, but don't make the mistake of thinking that all daddy-daughter dates have to expensive. Those times are supposed to be extraspecial, and that aspect is taken away when expensive dates become the norm. Most of the time, just going to the mall, to a restaurant, or fishing—depending on your child's personality—can do wonders for a girl's self-esteem. Just knowing that you love her enough to spend time with her will make her feel loved. Time spent with your daughter is more important than money spent on her.

7

What They See When They See You

When my firstborn was still pretty young, I had really long hair. It's not an exaggeration to say it went past midback. I had dreams of being a rock and roller, and it was part of my image. For the first couple years of her life, that was the norm. She would brush it and make daddy pretty with something like one thousand barrettes and hair ties. It was one of her favorite things to do!

About that time in my life, I was trying to make some decisions for my future. I realized I didn't really like having the long hair anymore, and I hadn't been in a band for at least four years, so I decided to cut it. I was a youth pastor, and I wanted to look respectable, so I figured I'd cut it relatively short and more in line with the style of the day.

It was a tough decision! I had long hair for a long time, but I felt like it was time for a change, so I figured I should go through with it before I chickened out. While my wife and I were enjoying our first weekend away after our child's birth, I decided on a whim to stop and chop it all off. Our daughter was at Grandma and Grandpa's house being spoiled, and I was ready to take a walk on the wild side. We drove to a local hair place, one of those you find in a strip mall and asked if they donated hair they cut to a charity like Locks of Love. When they said yes, I found myself in a position I hadn't been in for years, in a barber chair with some stranger about to cut off my flowing mane.

I had a moment of remorse as I sat there, apron tied around my neck to keep the hair off my clothes. I might have cried a little bit, but I went through with it because it was for a great cause, and I needed a change. It doesn't take long for two feet of hair to be cut clean from your head. It was a mix of feeling refreshed, relaxed, and a little saddened over my loss. I had forgotten how nice having a haircut can feel! As the hairstylist finished my new look, I decided to accept the change regardless of the outcome.

My decision to accept was short-lived as the shock of my new reflection began to sink in. What had I done? I had a thinning spot on top that I hadn't noticed when my hair was long. My neck grew about six inches too. And my face got fuller. I was looking at a complete stranger. I hadn't felt the wind blow on my neck for so long that I felt a little chilled in the eighty-degree weather. I asked my wife what she thought, and she said she liked it, but I wasn't sure. I didn't even look like me!

Shortly after the haircut, we made the hour-and-a-half trek to my in-laws to pick up our daughter. I was slightly surprised to see the terrified expression on her face when

I walked through the door. In my haste to cut my hair, I hadn't thought about how my child would react. I assumed she wouldn't even notice. Was I ever wrong. Not only had I terrified my baby; I was crushed by her reaction.

She couldn't figure out who this man was that sounded and acted like daddy but didn't look like him. I had become a stranger, and what was worse, Momma had brought him in like she didn't even notice he was the wrong guy! I could imagine the thoughts that were going through her little head, and I immediately felt regret at the decision to change my appearance. I wondered, briefly, if she'd ever hug me again or call me daddy. It was a sad hour or so before she began to trust her ears more than her eyes.

It's funny to me now, but in the moment, those irrational thoughts seemed to be the only possible outcome of my decision to get a haircut. I had become so used to her running and jumping into our arms when she hadn't seen us, even for a short time, that I thought I had scarred her forever. That the haircut would be the stumbling block for our relationship, and that she might never be able to see me in the same way again.

It didn't take long for that to become a distant memory. She still played with her barrettes in my hair, but she would complain that they didn't stay very well. Thank God that the foundation of the love we have for people isn't based on what's seen. I had to convince her for a moment that I was still the same guy, I just looked different; and eventually she accepted the fact that daddy was still daddy—he just had less hair. Her fear was based on what she saw, but her heart knew that I was the same guy who would sit and watch VeggieTales or play Barbies with her.

Our kids see us for who we really are. It isn't based on what we put forward for the world around us to see. No matter how we try to hide our true self from them, they see it. It's what they identify with. I've tried very hard from the beginning to be real with my children. They don't have to, or need to, know every intimate detail, but they know more than you think. If you aren't honest with them, their curiosity will drive them to look deeper, and when they discover you aren't who you portray yourself to be, that leads to deep wounds that take time to heal.

My children know I'm weak, and they know I have been wrong on occasion. They know they are important to me, and if I say we are going to do something, it takes a whole lot for me to go back on that word. They know that if I have to change plans, it's for a good reason, and I didn't decide to do it lightly because I want them to understand that, next to their mother, they are the most important thing I have been entrusted with in this life. I want them to see the real me and to know that I am striving to better myself every day. It makes it easier to teach them and help them through their own mistakes.

Bria

Different people see us in different ways. People see the image of ourselves that we show them, especially if they are not a part of our immediate family. Friends and even aunts and uncles and grandparents who don't live with or near you only see the image you show them. For example, if you are a fan of a certain television show, and you tell someone that but you don't tell them anything else, that is the only part of you that they know. Another way of looking at it could be like those close-up picture games. You only show one part of the image, even if it's really up close, and if you don't show them the rest, then that's the only part they see.

It's different with close family or even close friends. Family has a way of seeing the whole picture, no matter what you decide to show them. Like when a parent or child asks the other if something is wrong, even if there's hardly an intimation that something could be wrong. Family members can many times tell that something is wrong even when you are telling yourself that nothing is wrong. Family sees you in a different way than anyone else.

Many times, a child can see through their parent's guise of normality in a heartbeat. Children can interpret things that adults cannot hope to because their minds are open to more possibilities than the adults'. Children can tell when you are trying to avoid answering their questions even if they don't say anything.

Our families see us for who we truly are, whether we like it or not, especially children. However, it's not just children who see through disguises. Parents can see through them just as well, and that can scare kids. Here's some advice from a teenager: if you know that your child has done something, and they don't know that you know, tell them that you do—especially if the activity that you know of has happened more than once. Now if it isn't anything of consequence, this is not as big a deal; but if it is something that could in any way really lead to a downward spiral, sit down with them and talk about it. Be vulnerable with your kids.

Do not try to convince your child or children that you are perfect because we know you aren't. Sometimes when you admit it, it becomes easier for your child to accept it. Also, don't be afraid to cry. This is a hard one for dads. I know that you want to be strong, and I'm not saying you should cry in front of your kids about every single thing; however, do not be afraid to show them that you have weaknesses and that you are human. If something is emotionally moving, don't be afraid and try to choke back the tears for your kid's or your pride's sake. If anything, this kind of vulnerability with your children will make the relationship stronger rather than weaker.

Remember, your child will know more about you than you realize sometimes, just like you sometimes know more about them then they know. Don't be afraid to be honest and vulnerable with your kid or kids. It is important that they see that it is okay to cry and to swallow your pride. They already know that you are human, so you are imperfect. Don't ever try to convince them otherwise. Trust me; they will see through your facade of perfection every time.

8

Our Differences Make Us Stronger?

It is scary to me how much my children are like me. I feel bad for them. I do! I'm kinda weird, but in a good way! I remember my parents saying, "One day I hope you grow up and have kids who act just like you." Their wish came true! I have two girls, who act a little too much like me if you ask their mother. But I wouldn't change them at all!

In spite of our similarities though, it's our differences that really make them standout! It would be boring to have three people in the house with exact personalities, liking and doing everything the same way. There are areas in each of them where I've wished they might be a little more like me or their mom, but those are things that add to their uniqueness, and believe me, they are unique!

I am very proud of the individuality of my girls. The oldest is a dreamer with her head so far in the clouds that I worry she might not get enough oxygen. The youngest still dreams, but she's uberintelligent! You might say she's too smart for her own good!—like a mini-Einstein, without the whacked-out hair, and she's a she. Her older sister is really smart too! Both girls have incredible imaginations. They both love people and want to make sure everyone feels accepted. In fact, they are a lot like each other, maybe even more than they are like me and their mom. Still, they're as different as night and day.

Each responds to the same situation differently. If I gave them the same problem to solve, they'd both arrive at the right answer but probably take a different approach to get there. One is far more athletic than the other. One daydreams more than the other. Some of the differences are subtle, others are opposites and make you wonder if they are even related. It's the same when I compare each one to me or their mom. Many similarities, but a lot of differences too.

It's a healthy mix. I can't imagine our family would make it if we didn't each have our unique part to play. It's like each person has a unique gift that adds so much to the family dynamic.

When we were expecting our second, every one told us how truly different each would be, but I'm not sure I totally bought into the idea. I assumed proximity would create like beings, but it didn't. Each one is emotionally different. They deal differently with discipline, and each requires an individual approach. What works for one is almost certain to not work with the other. Their behavior is sometimes so different that it's hard to believe they used to share a bedroom; but other times, it's so similar you'd swear they were the same person.

Maybe our differences are so much more visible because of how similar we truly are. We assume that the other person will naturally react in the same manner we would react because we are so much alike. We almost forget that the other person is unique because our similarities tend to blur our individuality. It's like school uniforms or sports teams where everybody wins. If no one stands out, then no one is special.

I encourage my girls to be individuals, to celebrate their differences, and to allow their unique attributes to contribute to the whole. We were all made very different for a reason. We couldn't accomplish greatness if we were all cookie-cutter images of each other. We should challenge people to accept their uniqueness, rather than forcing them to conform to a predescribed image that removes the hope our individuality brings. It's those differences that challenge us to dream something greater than the status quo. Conformity doesn't take us to peace, rather, it leads to chaos.

Those differences are what leads a great thinker to rise above the norm and push through the doubt to achieve what they were told was impossible! Differences make athletes with extraordinary abilities and artists who paint with phenomenal depth and vivid imagery. They give poets and writers the ability to craft images in our minds from the words on a page, and help composers create beautiful memories that become the soundtrack of our lives. Differences are good, make no mistake!

If we all were the same, there would be no reason to try. Our differences push us to be something greater than we've imagined. They are the mechanics that put our dreams to flight. Without them, life would be very boring and predictable.

So set aside your differences. Celebrate them and realize that they aren't meant to cause argument or division; they are the connecting pieces of life's puzzle. The differences in those around us are the very things that make us who we are when we accept others as they are. They make us stronger. They really do!

Bria

Thank God that my dad and I are not exactly the same! The world could not handle two of either of us! My dad and I do have a lot in common, but we are by no means exactly the same. Imagine, if my dad and I were exactly the same, what a boring and utterly pointless relationship ours would be.

I am a girl; so I do have some girly interests like makeup, clothes, and boys. Now I am not very absorbed in any of these, but these things do go through my head now and then. I have some minor (okay, sometimes major) fangirl (if you don't know what this is, ask your daughter) moments sometimes when I hear a song or watch a stupid television show that I may or may not be obsessed with, which may or may not have a boy in it who I may or may not think is cute. My dad, being much more calm and collected, reserves any reactions like these for sports games—to yell at the referee or cheer when his favorite team executes an amazing play— or for video games that he has either waited a long time to play or gotten irritated at for glitching.

An important point to make is that these differences do not weaken our relationship. They actually strengthen it. Think about it: if you are putting together a football team, you don't want to draft a team made up entirely of quarterbacks or safeties. You need a variety of players with a variety of skills to be successful.

A family is like a team. Everyone has an important part to play, and everyone needs different skills to play his or her part. When two people are different, they can learn from their differences. If two people are the same, then they can't learn anything from each other; and that is what the father-daughter relationship is about: your daughter learning from you, and you learning from her. I have learned so much from my dad, and apparently he has learned things from me, because we are different. If we were exactly the same, there would be nothing that either of us could learn from the other.

9

We Do Have Common Interests

I'm not sure if it's a blessing or a curse, but my daughters are a lot like me. They like the same things from movies to sports; we enjoy spending time together doing and watching the same things.

My youngest daughter likes football a lot! We like the same teams, which is nice on game day! We celebrate their victories and fret their defeats. I never asked her to like football; after all, she is a young lady. Offsides and holding are penalties she needs to remember for dating, not sports. She came to like it on her own, and she prides herself in knowing a little more about football than the casual fan, male or female!

We like the same movies. We both love to sing and have probably sung nearly every song about a certain mermaid or a lion cub hundreds of times. It's not just about my girls liking the same things that I do. I encourage them to find their own identities and likes; they just happen to be similar in a lot of ways.

At first, it was weird to me that two little girls acted so much like little boys. I was worried that I might be hurting their development. Both of the girls like girly things, but they like the things that are typically attributed to boys too. It's okay! No harm has come to them, and they have expanded my idea of what's interesting too.

Common interests are not a bad thing as long as a child is given a chance to decide for themselves. Too many parents try to relive their glory days through their kids. It's not only sad, it's embarrassing to the child and the adult, though the latter usually has no idea and doesn't realize that they are making a total fool of themselves.

Encourage them to decide for themselves the style of music they like, what they do for fun, the movies they enjoy, and so on. It will solidify the relationship you have, especially if you place value on those things that maybe just don't make sense to you. It's okay for them to like different things as long as you make an effort to understand what they are involved in.

As parents, we often make one of two mistakes: we either force our kids into something we want for them, or we have a blind indifference to raising them. Whether you let them raise themselves, or you try to mold them into your perfect ideal of a child, you are creating a wall that will one day separate you from your kids. That wall might take years to tear down. It might always be, between you and them, a constant reminder to the child of feeling that they've failed in some way.

It's far better to support and encourage them to be themselves. Get excited about what they get excited about! In return, they will do the same. My girls and I still love to sit and watch certain movies we've watch over and over again. They aren't the typical movies you'd expect a girl to love, but I've invested in them by watching certain "princess movies" until my eyes were about to pop out of my head and my ears nearly bled. It was worth every animation-filled minute!

Sometimes they act a little bit like boys, but they are all girls, filled with emotional roller coasters that loop and twist more than the latest thrill ride at Cedar Point! They like to fish and hunt, but they also like it when I take the time to do a cold-water french manicure for them while watching one of our favorite action flicks!

It's okay! Someday some lucky young man will be blessed with a young lady who can cast a line, cook a meal, and get dressed up like a princess when necessary. We may have a lot in common, but it's our differences that make us stronger and help us to see the value in each other!

Bria

I have been predominantly raised by my dad for most of my life. This fact can be pretty clearly seen in my interests and likes. I take after my dad quite a bit. I am a tomboy. Now don't get me wrong. I am a girl; I still like to put on makeup, do my hair, and listen to boy bands every now and again. I do have moments like this, but not as often as my sister who took more after my mom in many areas. I am not saying that I do not have crazy fangirl moments now and again, but I am not a typical girl. I have never been completely opposed to hunting or getting my hands dirty. I like to go fishing with my dad and go to car shows now and then. I have been a nerd my whole life. I was a sci-fi and fantasy nerd before it was cool. I like to tell people that (apart from Veggie Tales) I was practically raised on Star Wars and Lord of the Rings.

Some of the things I pointed out above may be kind of normal for girls now, but they weren't really when I was little. My dad raised me to be a hard-working, Jedi-loving girl. My dad has said before that he would have liked to have a boy after my sister and me, but he didn't get that far from one when they had me. I like to go to sports games (even if I just follow that game and not the entire year for a team: that is my sister's job), watch movies where something or somebody gets blown up at some point, climb up high mountains, and explore dark caves.

My dad and I have a lot in common. Other than those surface things, like movie genres and activities, we both love to serve people, which is another thing I got from him. I love to act crazy to try to get a middle-schooler or little kid to laugh and, better yet, open up to receive Jesus. I love to do service projects and other outreach things, like going on food runs for the church's food pantry, or getting food from the food pantry for someone. These are all things that I have gotten from my dad.

Now don't think that just because your daughter takes more after Mom than she does from Dad you don't have anything in common. Honestly, that is a cop-out answer that seems like you are just trying to find an easy way out of bonding with your daughter. I guarantee you that you and your daughter have some common interests, and they should not be hard to spot. If you can't think of anything, you aren't thinking nearly hard enough, or paying nearly enough, attention. It may not seem like you and your daughter share any common interests, but you absolutely do. Just pay attention, and they will be incredibly clear if they aren't already.

My dad and I share many common interests, ranging from types of entertainment to types of adventure to ways of serving people. We are by no means exactly alike. Thank God for that! No one could handle two of my dad (or of me)! Also, that would be incredibly boring, and there really wouldn't be much of a purpose to our relationship. However, we do have a lot in common. Part of that comes from my dad having been a stay-at-home dad for most of my life; but part of it is that I am just like him. Remember, don't give up hope if you don't immediately see something you have in common. There is at least something there, and there are almost definitely multiple common interests that you and your daughter share. Once you have identified those things (or if you already have identified them), use them to your advantage. Use those things to spend time with your daughter and bond with her. She will thank you, and you will thank yourself.

10

Getting There Is Half the Fun

Making memories doesn't require that you spend a fortune! Often the destination isn't as important as the drive. How we get where we're going and what we do along the way builds as many memories as the most extravagant points of interest.

Being a youth pastor in my spare time (because being a husband and a dad comes first), my summers, falls, and occasional springs have been filled with trips to youth camps, ski resorts, camping in beautiful locations and theme parks. From Disneyland to Cedar Point or the Great Smoky Mountains to beach getaways in Destin, we often talk more about the time spent traveling than the actual time on location.

The road makes memories that last forever. It's where vehicle breakdowns lead to impromptu photo ops with the police or crazy dance parties on the side of the road. Great talks and fun sing-alongs, the miles we put behind us build the excitement for what's to come! With each passing moment, new memories are made, and new friendships are born. Unexpected stops lead to misadventures that undoubtedly spawn tales of woe for years to come.

Whether it be with the students I've mentored or my own family, road trips are what we talk about when we reminisce. Not because the places we go are boring. Sometimes they are downright expensive, but the adventure happens on the journey. Fortunately, my own children have had the opportunity to accompany me on many of the journeys throughout the years and have had a pivotal part to play in the memories made.

When we're on vacation, it can be so easy to go into our separate areas and focus on what we like to do; but on the drive, we're forced to be close to each other. We could put in headphones or play a game on our cell phone, but we miss the best parts of the journey. Like the time we played the alphabet game in the Upper Peninsula of Michigan; it was one of the longest games ever because there are places on the back roads, and even on some of the main roads, where there are no signs for miles, and no cars to be seen. It was slow, but we laughed about it and talk about it to this day.

My daughters are in their teens, and we still play the alphabet game. We talk for hours about their favorite shows or books and laugh as we discuss the details of past trips. We sing "Silly Songs" and the latest Disney soundtrack until we hear them in our sleep. We quote our favorite movie scripts, and when we get tired of that, we start all over again. The drive is rarely boring because we engage each other, and that's why it's often my favorite part of the trip.

In today's fast-paced life with school, church, work, and extracurricular activities, it can be rare to have them in such a captive setting. When you do, make the most of it! Talk for hours about nothing, remembering they won't always be there in the backseat, listening to stories of how you and their mom fell in love. It's a great time to speak into their lives and to discuss issues they face every day.

I'll be the first to admit, sometimes it's nice to just drive in peace and quiet. I like those moments when they are sleeping, and I can get a few extra miles in between bathroom stops, but I eventually long for the sound of laughter and, sometimes, meaningless conversation. They love it too! We talk, and as we talk, the walls come down, and our relationships become stronger.

The time spent on vacation is fun too! Don't get me wrong. Disney World is amazingly, magically fun no matter how old you are; and watching the sun rise or set in the mountains is a breathtaking site that needs to be shared with those you love. We experience life together and then revisit the moment in the car as we travel back to wherever we are laying our heads that night.

The journey doesn't have to be long or extravagant, it just needs to be experienced together. Those memories are a strong bond that hold a fond place in each of us. They help us come through difficult times and give us things to help us cope in moments of grief. We think back on the memories of time spent with the ones we've lost and wish we had taken more time while they were with us. Don't give yourself a reason to regret; make the most of each day and each opportunity. Simple ones are often more meaningful than the most expensive trips. Go somewhere and experience life together. It will build memories that last far longer than the eighteen to twenty years we spend parenting them under our roof.

I think back to some of my fondest memories as a child and they revolve around time spent with family. Sometimes we were on an overnight road trip, other times we were taking a short daycation, but the experience helped me through some of the most tumultuous times in my life. I have since taken my family to travel some of those same roads so that we can share the experiences I've cherished for so long, making new memories that reside next to the old.

Building a history with your kids doesn't have to cost a lot. Don't put so much pressure on yourself. Find something that you all enjoy and spend time together, experiencing all that life has to offer. After all, the time we have is relatively short and best spent encountering adventures—some small, others large—with the ones we love. We are meant to live life to the fullest!

Bria

Some of my fondest memories took place on road trips. I remember the things that happened on the way to a long-awaited vacation destination as much as I do about the destination. In the car on the way, there are things that happen that could not happen at the destination.

For example, a few years ago, we took a family vacation to Disney World for Christmas. My mom was not with my dad, sister, and me in the car because of schedule conflicts on this particular trip. The three of us had left the house as soon as I had gotten home from school. The van was all packed, and we were ready to go. We had decided that we would not attempt the entire drive without stopping, so we stopped Friday night at a little hotel in Georgia and completed the venture on Saturday afternoon. I remember my dad making fun of me for constantly squinting at the sun, no matter how bright it was. I would look out the windshield, and after a few seconds I would look away with watery eyes. We stopped at a bunch of little places on the way, because we weren't in a hurry; we were enjoying the drive.

Another example would be our countless summer road trips. One year, we decided to stop one day on the way back from visiting relatives in Michigan and spend the day at Holiday World. That night, in and of itself, was an adventure. We spent hours driving around the Santa Claus, IN area, looking for an affordable hotel. We went down several back roads that did not have a lot of street lights. We drove through little towns until we finally found something. Before we found the hotel we ended up staying in, I searched the Internet for a cheap hotel. As I was searching, I came across something. However, it turned out this location was in the Canadian Rockies. When I told my dad this, Lexy chimed in, saying, "But I don't want to go to Canadada." We laughed and laughed and laughed. As I previously stated, we did find a hotel; but I remember this trip mostly by the memories made on the way to the park, not the time we spent at the park.

Last summer, we took a trip to Northern Michigan. We had to make memories on the road, because there was nothing else to do except sleep as we drove for hours down a never-changing, never-turning road. We stopped at several parks and little stores on the way up and back. It was a fun trip, but probably the most driving we ever had to do on a trip.

For a vacation to be memorable, it doesn't have to be expensive; it doesn't even have to be long. Just a day or two at a state park can be fun. Also, remember not to underestimate the car rides. Those are the times when random sing-alongs and in-your-seat dance parties take place. The times when you are a little bit tired but can't sleep are when you make the craziest memories, so don't just wait until you reach the destination to have fun.

11

Memories

I have made a concerted effort to impact my daughter's lives. Not with a bunch of stuff, but with opportunities to build memories that form the building blocks of our relationship now and in years to come. It's the memories that hold us together when times are tough. I don't want my children sitting down in ten or twenty years, wishing that they had gotten to spend more time with me. They are one of the greatest gifts God has blessed me with in this life. I would rather not work solely for the acquisition of things. There is nothing more important to acquire than the heart of your child!

You capture their heart by imagining with them. Don't be afraid to let your child see you act a little silly from time to time. It won't ruin your ability to bring correction; it will enhance it. The memories you create today are building trust for your relationship. Being willing to act goofy or show them that you have dreams too builds a strong bond between you.

We have memories aplenty! Some of my favorites involve my children absolutely making me look ridiculous. It takes a strong man and a lot of love to let your daughters do your hair or your nails. It takes even more love to do their nails for them. Believe me, the impact of such a simple gesture isn't easily forgotten.

An article printed in July 2013 in the UK Daily Mail cites a survey conducted by Virgin Holidays and Universal Studios Orlando claims that the average family spends less than eight hours each week engaging in activity together. On weekdays families spend about a half an hour together. Seven out of ten reported that much of that time included, "time spent sitting in front of the television in silence." It goes on to say that many families schedule vacations for the sake of, "enjoying some real time with family beyond the demands of daily life." Consider the source. Of course Universal Studios Orlando is going to produce a survey that favors taking a vacation. The numbers are still alarming. When I compare it to my typical evenings with family the survey has a great deal of truth. It stresses the need to be intentional with the time we do have.

I think many times as parents, we are so consumed with being respected and obeyed that we forget how it feels when someone takes interest in something we like to do. It's a big moment when someone we care about makes us the center of attention. I have found that respect comes much easier when people know that you are willing to set aside your agenda, so in that moment their desire is the focus.

When I think back to my own childhood, it isn't the lessons my mom and dad taught me through threats that have stuck. It's the ones that came in a moment of weakness or when they showed me that I had value. I wanted to do the things that they liked because they were willing to do the things I wanted to do occasionally. Something as simple as catching worms to go fishing the next day. I was so excited because I knew that when the sprinklers came on, the worms would come to the surface, and if we took the time to catch them, then we surely would take the time to use them!

Many of the memories you build won't even mean that much to you, but it will make a world of difference for your child. It doesn't have to be costly! In fact, I've found the less you spend on the moment, the more relaxed and natural those memories are formed. Sitting and talking, walking and listening as they dream about what the future holds. Some of the best memories are made in the simplest setting.

Those memories will be like the change in your pocket when times get rough. You'll fall back on them. It's much better to have established positive moments to reflect on when the inevitable times of trial arise. Better to have the memory of times shared, moments of achievement witnessed, and victories or defeats shared than the lack of moments of real significance. Work can wait. Your child is more important than any job and far more valuable than any possession on earth.

As adults, we don't put enough value in the small things. We are caught up with what we have to do to provide for our families. We are running so fast toward the big picture that we forget to take time and enjoy the journey. The greatest achievements in life are meaningless if there is no one to share the experience with. A child gets more out of fifteen minutes spent with them each day than they get from the work put in to provide them with all the latest electronics and clothes. They want those things, but it's typically because we program them to want them.

Because of our absence, we make up for it by giving them what they ask for instead of what they need. Your time is the best gift because it translates into a central idea within your child: I am important to my dad. All the money in the world won't translate the same way. There are a lot of unhappy, unhealthy young people out there who feel unloved but have everything they've ever wanted.

Kids are manipulative. If we program them to believe that we give something because we love them, they will exploit it! If you've never been one to spend much time with your kids, and suddenly you do, they will fight you over it. But deep down, they really crave our participation in their lives. They don't need us to be their friend or to try to recapture our youth through them. They need us to love them and cherish them, and the best way to show that to a child is by spending time with them, investing in their identity.

No matter how much our kids look like us, talk like us, and act like us, they aren't us. Kids want to know that we love them enough to value who they are, that their opinions have value. When we build memories with them by investing the necessary time, we create bond that can overcome all the noise that attempts to distract them. It can't be done casually; it must be intentional! Memories matter, create them often!

Bria

Memories are the things that make up any relationship. Without memories, a relationship would not grow. A father needs to be there to create memories with his kids so that when he can't be there, they have those memories to fall back on so the relationship can remain strong. Memories need to be created when they are young and as they grow. The more good memories a child has of their father, the stronger the relationship will be.

Think of it this way: memories are the materials to build a relationship, which for now will be a house. Different materials will make different quality houses. Poor materials will make a weak house that will crumble the minute strong winds and rains come. A house made of strong materials will outlast the storms. There may be some damage, but that can be fixed. Also, you have to have materials to build the house in the first place. The more materials you have, the bigger the house can be, the stronger it can be. If you don't have the materials, you can't build the house.

Memories are the same way. The more memories you make, the stronger the relationship will be; the better and stronger they are, the stronger the relationship will be when storms come.

The memories won't all be good, though. No matter how hard you try or how much you wish, there will always be hard times between you two. But that is normal. It can even be healthy. I have some memories of my dad that I am not overly fond of, but I do not focus on them. I don't focus on them because we made up. The point is not to just give your child everything she wants; it's to give her what she needs, and sometimes you will have disagreements. Sometimes you are right, and sometimes your child is. The key is to be open-minded. Another thing is to apologize when you realize that you are wrong or when you handle a situation in an inappropriate way. If you apologize, many times your child will catch on and start apologizing for things.

Every relationship is made up of memories, and some memories are good, while others are bad. They key to building a lasting, healthy relationship is to create as many happy memories as you can and to try to fix the bad ones as best as you can so that they don't spoil the good things.

Going back to the house analogy; a house can be renovated, and you can build on to it. Don't stop making memories when your child becomes a teenager. You can keep improving upon the relationship and make it last even longer.

Also, if you haven't already started making good memories with your daughter, and you're reading this and thinking, It's too late, you are wrong. It may be a bit harder for you to build a really good long-lasting relationship, but it is never too late. As I just said, a house can be renovated. It just takes a little more time and work because you have to take out the old and bring in the new. So don't ever think it's too late for you to build a strong relationship with your daughter because it never is.

12

Shadow Dancing

Game time holds fond memories for me. As a kid, my grandparents would teach me card games like Garbage and Peek-No-Peek. My aunt and uncle were fond of dominoes and Balderdash. My favorite part of family get-togethers came after the meal, when we would come together and play a game.

Sometimes the competition was intense, but it was always fun! Rarely did anyone ever step away angry, we were usually laughing so hard because of some answer or comment someone made in the moment. It felt good to see my parents, grandparents, aunts, and uncles in a different setting, less disciplinarian, more human.

From time to time, we'd get carried away, but we always looked forward to those friendly family competitions. From softball at the family reunion to badminton in my grandma's backyard to a heated game of Hungry Hippos amongst the cousins, those moments of family rivalry were some of the more memorable of my childhood.

I still like to play games as often as possible. The time spent playing sparks conversation that leads to laughter. We relive those memories sometimes days after, laughing nearly as hard as we did in the moment. It's good for our kids to see us with our guard down from time to time. It solidifies the relationship between a parent and child. Laughter is like glue. It creates a bond that isn't broken easily.

The problem comes when we get so busy that we forget the joy that comes from the simplest games. We become consumed and just don't feel like playing! We're tired, so we say we'll play tomorrow. Tomorrow usually is just as busy, so we push it back another day, then another. Tomorrow never comes. It's always one day away. We never get there because we aren't intentional with our time.

I've often thought about how much time I waste in the course of a day. If I replaced some of that downtime with a game of cards or a maybe some chess, how much more productive would I be? I think we devalue the benefit of play because we get so busy, or we think it's not the adult thing to do. But what's wrong with splashing in a puddle from time to time, or chasing your kids across the yard trying to pounce on each others shadows? We don't do it because we're afraid we'll look silly.

We don't want to look silly because we're afraid we will lose the respect of those around us. We think people are watching all the time and, the truth is, they are. What they see isn't a silly, immature nut, who shouldn't be allowed around children, much less be given the opportunity to parent. They see a mom or a dad who loves their kids so much that they are willing to invest in them the most precious commodity we can give a child: our time.

I am so thankful for the moments my aunt and uncle opened their home to play games like Dominoes or Scattergories. They invested a great deal in me during those nights when we created funny definitions for nonsense words like balderdash. They didn't have to play, but I think they really enjoyed those times. I know I did. It's their example, and the example of my parents and grandparents, that I try to follow now.

There are some nights I just don't feel like playing. Lord knows that sometimes Monopoly feels like penance rather than something we do for fun. Truth be told, I don't ever remember regretting taking a moment to stop and play a game with my kids. No matter how busy I am, I think there is something therapeutic about taking an hour to focus on them in the midst of the chaos of everyday life. It helps me feel younger and brings me joy that few things can match. Even though I don't like to lose, I enjoy their reactions when they win.

A game can break up the most monotonous road trip and bring a smile to a disappointing day. It leads to moments of honest conversation and reflection; it brings laughter and joy. Dreams are shared as countries are conquered and hotels are built. It's not insignificant, it's crucial to your relationship and to your child's well being. Play a game whenever time allows, and sometimes when it won't. You certainly will not regret the smile on your child's face.

Don't be afraid to make up your own games either! Be creative and enjoy the moments you have. It isn't really the length of time spent playing. It's the fact that you've made the time to play in the first place. Don't let lack of time stop you from a quick game of hide-and-seek or the occasional outbreak of Nerf darts flying through the air as you look for your Nerf gun and run to cover. My family still talks about the battles of past, or the time we lost one of our kids in the clothing section at Walmart because she decided to play a little hide-and-seek in the clothes racks. It scared me, but you had to laugh when she poked her little head through the clothes and said boo!

Games are time-consuming, but they will fill your child's mind with good memories for years to come. Establish the pattern early so it doesn't seem like you're overcompensating for time lost. It doesn't have to be complex. Some of the most fun is had playing the simplest game. In the end, the thing that matters is you took time and gave it to your child and you shared a laugh together.

Bria

My dad and I have played many conventional games over the years, such as Risk, chess, Monopoly, and Trivial Pursuit. Other games that we played were not so conventional. We would run around, trying to step on each other's shadows. We have played tag in the car on road trips. We loved to play with Barbies, and I loved to put every single miscellaneous barrette and hair tie that I could find in my dad's hair. My dad can probably recall the several games we used to play better than I, but I can pull a few from my memory because those were times my daddy spent time with me; and those times forever shaped my life and our relationship.

Even now, I love to play games with my dad from time to time. We play everything, from card games like Apples to Apples and Nertz, to board games like Risk, to video games like Disney Universe. We love to play games together, especially when we can laugh together, which is basically every time we play a game.

We are a very competitive family. We compete with each other and other people. Even just the other day, my dad and I were on a daddy-daughter date at Chili's. They had these little screens on the tables with games on them. We looked at the games and immediately jumped on the trivia game. My mom often says that my dad and I are crazy because we can remember every little detail about a movie after seeing it twice. We love to show off our skill and random knowledge at home and in public. It makes for some really funny conversations and memories, especially when our memories differ. The point is no matter if we are running through a parking lot, trying to step on each other's shadows, or trying to strategically take over a flat cardboard world, we love to have fun and spend time with each other. Sometimes we may get irritated with each other, but we love to bond over games, whether it be something made up or copyrighted.

13

Testing Boundaries

I have to say my girls are pretty good, nearly perfect, but they have their moments! Still, they are nothing like me when I was a kid. I would push, poke, and prod my way as close as I could come to their limit, trying to stretch my boundaries to the breaking point. If it were a test, I'd have failed. As much as I get aggravated with them, they are far from the way I was, and for that I am thankful! We have, at least in a small way, managed to avoid completely fulfilling the curse of my parents that I would have a kid who acted exactly the way I did!

From time to time though, my daughters will push the limits. From cell phones to TV time, our boundaries have been tested. It's funny how times have changed, but kids still do the same things. Struggling against the limits to try and prove their independence is definitely not a new thing after all. It's just new to the parent who is being challenged at the moment. Somehow we forget all the boundaries we've pushed. Out of fear that they will do the things we did, we clamp down ever tighter, only pushing them harder to stretch the limits we've placed.

I think it's really a part of the growing-up process, but I don't like it! I can't stand thinking that someday my little princess will be at that place where there is a choice between two paths in front of her. My hope is she'd take the one that is well-marked with the arrows I've placed there as a guide to direct her. But I fear the mystery of the unmarked path will entice her to push right through the barrier and test what was set up to protect her.

I can't make their decisions for them. No one made mine for me. I have to trust that they will make wise choices. But they can't if I don't provide them with accurate information. It can't always be about the negative consequences either because we humans have a tendency to want to disprove what's generally accepted as truth. We believe that it won't be like that for us, so we push the limit only to find ourselves fighting the same struggle we were warned would come.

I remember my daughters burning themselves when I had warned them something was hot and it shouldn't be touched. They learned their lesson, but it could have been so much easier. I imagine parents throughout history have struggled with the same thing and thought their children would be different, only to discover the hard way that we as people seem to naturally push against anything that holds us back.

The boundaries we set are important, but we need not be naive in thinking that our kids won't challenge them. Even the almost perfect child will face moments when they question what they've been told their whole lives. It has happened throughout history, and history is constantly repeating itself. Like history is trying to show us our boundaries, but we just have to prove that it will be different for us. Sound familiar?

We are like an adventurer who comes upon a gorge in the jungle crossed by a rickety old bridge. The signs say danger, do not cross, but we choose to ignore the fraying old ropes and broken, sometimes missing, boards because we don't want to be told that we can't do something. It annoys us and pushes us to risk our very lives to prove that what we were told couldn't or shouldn't be done not only can be done, but we can do it better than anyone who has gone before. The screaming voices telling us stop often are the very thing that fuel us to push past the warning signs and barricades. We're often so far out on the bridge that we can't turn back when the rope unravels. We have to decide in that moment to move forward, turn back, or stay still, hoping it doesn't all crash down around us.

We become embarrassed and hide our failures because we don't want to hear, "I told you so." Often, our kids feel the same way that we would if we had made the same mistake. The fear of repercussion leads us to hide those things and often puts us in a position where we make many more mistakes as a result. It is so much better to be open with your kids knowing that, because you set the boundary, chances are it will be tested. We never quite get past that little child who eyes Mom and Dad to see what they will do as they reach for the cookie or the stove, disregarding the warnings of impending danger or punishment.

It has been this way since the beginning!—"Eat from any tree except this one." What happened? We tend to give into temptations more frequently than resisting them. That's why it's so important to train a child in the way they should go. They won't stray far from it, but there's a good chance they will stray a little bit. We shouldn't be shocked or appalled when mistakes happen! That only increases the embarrassment felt by our kids. We are curious by nature, and when left to ourselves, we tend to stray far more easily than when we have been informed of the bigger picture by someone whom we trust. Through a proper parent-child relationship, we have the influence that is necessary to affect positive decisions and direction in the life of our child. If we don't inform them, believing that our child would never do those things, we push them to choose every stumbling blocks that hold us back and destroy us if we aren't careful.

Boundaries are important! They are necessary, but they shouldn't be blindly set, assuming that they will never be tested or stretched. Setting them with the knowledge that they will be tested keeps us aware and observant of the warnings that are there if we only recognize them.

Boundaries don't keep trouble from coming, they hold us from plummeting to the depths, if those around us play their part and see where we get a little too close to the edge. Kids will be kids, humans will be humans. If our tendency is to do the opposite of what we're told, what difference does a barrier make? It's just one more obstacle to go around as we approach what has piqued our interest.

It's the same for us as adults. That's why affairs happen and marriages fail because curiosity leads us to go past the boundaries we've accepted for ourselves. If adults can't deal with the same temptations that our kids struggle with, how can we expect them to make wise choices? Getting mad because they haven't learned from our mistakes is ridiculous! It's naive! Be a constant guide—engage your kids! Check your borders and boundaries regularly and look for the signs that trouble is encroaching. Be aware of where your kids are and love them through their mistakes. You made some too, probably the same ones! You aren't the failure. You would only be a failure if you didn't do something in the midst of the situation. If you throw up your hands and give up, you're in danger of losing not just your child, but yourself as well. Love them through it. It never fails!

Bria

When you were a kid, bedtime was a really big thing, or at least it was when I was little. Everybody would talk about their bedtime and compare the times to see who got to stay up the latest. Someone telling you that they had no bedtime was insane. That person was immediately one of the coolest kids ever.

Not only was having a later bedtime important for growing up, but children feel honor-bound to continue the valiant fight to push bedtime back as late as possible. Many different strategies are used: arguing with parents, keeping quiet and hoping they either won't notice the time or forget you were there, praying for every living and nonliving thing you can think of and insisting that they be prayed for in order, and especially, later in their career, sneaking up and trying to watch whatever Mom and Dad are watching from around the corner without getting caught.

These shenanigans are just an example of one of the many ways children test boundaries. They want to see what they can get away with. It's like they think about a rule, How can I bend this rule and get away with it? I know! I'll do this and see what happens. Then they go and carry out their self-assigned missions for the good of little kids everywhere.

Testing boundaries is a part of human nature that we may think we can outgrow, but we never really do. In high school, the bending of rules is an epidemic. At school, if kids have to wear their ID cards around their neck, some either don't wear them at all or they just wear a lanyard to see if they get caught. Some pull out their phones and hide them under the desk while they text someone. People know the rules, but it just gives us some sort of inner satisfaction to break them, or at least bend them.

This is very true in the father-daughter relationship. We both test each other's boundaries all the time. Many times we do it more than we think we do. With teenage girls, a lot of the time it is just the little things like how long will they let us watch TV or sit playing on our phones. We ask if we can do things at the last second, even if we have been instructed numerous times to plan ahead. As a dad, it is your job to test some of your daughter's boundaries, to push her to help her grow. Now there are some things like diaries and things like that, that if they are not causing any harm, should not be tested. Certain benign privacies like that should be respected. This applies to siblings as well.

There are also many unspoken boundaries in a relationship. Unspoken boundaries tend to be things that should be obvious enough that they shouldn't need to be stated directly. These could include simple things, like not going into a room without knocking first. Also, certain things could be very specific to a single person, things like not eating certain people's food without expressly asking first, or not bringing up certain people or things that would upset a specific person. Unspoken boundaries can be slightly harder to identify, but if the person is your child, and you have been thoroughly involved in his or her life, it should not be too difficult.

Boundaries are set to protect people, whether it be the person the boundary is applied to, or the person creating the boundary, or both. Testing boundaries is a part of human nature, and sometimes it can be a little beneficial to test boundaries, but sometimes they should just be left alone. The hard thing is listening and identifying the boundaries, including the unspoken ones, and determining just how imperative a specific boundary is. Once the boundary is identified, respect it, but don't just let a bunch of boundaries get built up between you and your little girl.

14

Frustrations

When our frustrations get the best of us, we often find ourselves preparing to apologize for something we're about to do or say. As a dad, I find my frustrations with my girls often stem from a lack of understanding or poor communication. Not on my part! Well, sometimes on my part, but usually on theirs.

Have you ever had one of those conversations with someone where you felt like you had broken everything down to the finest of details, short of drawing a picture, and they still didn't get it? You show them how to do something countless times, and they still don't understand. You begin to wonder if they secretly film you, pulling your hair out as you go over the fine points of whatever task it is you've set them to do. Do they enjoy seeing you turn red while you bite your tongue, only to turn around and do it yourself because you can't be bothered going over the process again?

I've gone to bed with a sore tongue a number of times. I think we all find ourselves in that spot from time to time. Usually, our impatience in the moment because of the demands placed on us only serves to further stress the situation. How many times do you have to show someone how to load the dishwasher or sort the laundry or clean the gutters? It seems like a simple process! I think we lose site of some things when we become responsible adults.

Being a kid is hard! You're changing constantly. People are urging you to grow up and figure out what you want to do with your life. You have school, friends, work, family all demanding your time! Throw in church or sports, and you have little time for yourself, let alone learning the proper way to cut the grass. When you were a kid, no one expected you to do your laundry or wash the dishes; they told you that you weren't old enough. When did you become "old enough?" You didn't even get a letter welcoming you to the club! One moment, you were playing with your dolls or your action figures, and the next you were being asked to scrub the floor in the bathroom.

I think we could limit our frustrations with each other if we would make a sincere effort to see the situation from the other's perspective. It helps me to understand the reactions I sometimes get even if I don't like it! It's not okay for my girls to react that way, but maybe my approach lead to the situation and their frustration. Communication is so important in relationships, but we rarely give it the time or attention needed.

Try a little experiment the next time you are having a conversation with someone. Consciously make note of how quickly and how often your mind drifts to topics other than what the conversation is about. For most of us, it happens frequently and faster than we would like to admit. We put it off on how busy we are, or being preoccupied with responsibilities, like work, even other relationships!

We aren't good listeners! Being a good listener is essential to being a good communicator. While we're looking for some way to contribute to the conversation, we miss half of what's being communicated! This leads to frustration for both parties in the discussion! If we could find a way to focus, maybe we could avoid a lot of the frustrations life brings.

If my girls are anything like me, it's no wonder they need to be told over and over again how and when to do things. They may pick up a little bit of what I'm saying, but it's mixed with song lyrics and homework, not to mention the latest bit of information from the "who likes who" conversation that day at school! It's still frustrating, but I get it. Maybe if I engaged them a little better while explaining what I need them to do, I wouldn't have to repeat myself as often.

When it comes down to it, that's one of the most frustrating things I have faced as a parent. Maybe even more frustrating than their bickering and fighting, but not much. I think part of being a family is learning to love each other in spite of those things that frustrate us.

Remembering that we all have our moments helps. I frustrate my wife on a regular basis, sometimes intentionally, but typically because I don't think through things the same way she does. Those same differences that make us great as a family are the little needles of aggravation that slowly work their way under our skin until they become so irritating, we explode.

My daughters are different from me, and that's the problem. I need to be able to accept their differences and learn what works with each person I deal with on an individual basis. What works for me probably won't work for them. That's why we need to develop strong relationships. Our relationships help us to understand what makes the other person tick! When we know what motivates another person, we can explain things in a way that works for them, and some of the frustrations we struggle with can be avoided. Because they are different, they each process things differently than I do and differently than the other. I can't use a cookie-cutter approach that leads to more aggravation!

No, I need to learn how to present things to each of my girls in a way that appeals to them individually. The only way I can possibly do that is to know their hearts and how they think. Understanding how they process what I'm telling them helps me to package what I'm saying in the most effective way. And though there will still be frustrating moments, they don't happen as frequently as they could. Adding to that, the idea that I frustrate people regularly too; in fact, I've been frustrating people my whole life helps me to not be so quick to allow my frustrations to push me to the point of losing my temper.

That's the danger of frustration. It pushes us to respond in ways that we wish later we hadn't. Identifying the things that trigger it, and recognizing that you've had more than enough are important keys to keeping your frustrations from pushing you over the edge. Sometimes, walking away is the only thing you can do. It's better than saying something you'll regret later. I've heard myself say things my parents said to me that I said I would never say to my kids, and that made me even more irritated.

It's not easy raising two teenagers, whether they are boys, girls, or one of each! Frustration will happen! There is no avoiding it. Add the dynamic of your spouse to the equation, and you're sure to have an occasional moment where you question your sanity and the sanity of those around you. Learning how to handle those moments is key to sustaining lasting relationships that endure through the hard times that will come!

Every person in your family is different, but the way those pieces fit together is what makes the puzzle complete. You can't force the pieces to come together. Smashing them into a spot they aren't formed for damages that piece. Discover how the pieces come together naturally, and you'll have the picture your family is intended to create. Frustration will come, but when each piece knows its unique part in the puzzle, you will hold together through the most trying times.

Bria

As a teenager, I am easily frustrated. My parents will ask me to do something, or my sister will come into my room without knocking, and I will blow up. It can be over the simplest of things. I don't know why I get so frustrated so easily, but it just seems to happen. Now I am not trying to excuse my behavior. I have even physically winced before when I have slammed a door or yelled at my sister. I don't always apologize right away, and sometimes I don't apologize at all. However, there are times that I find myself saying something, and in the same breath I am apologizing for whatever I said.

I do not enjoy being frustrated at anyone. I do not like to yell at my sister, but sometimes it just comes out, and most of the time the frustration isn't even directed at her. One big thing that I am guilty of doing is getting frustrated, mumbling under my breath, doing what I was asked with an atrocious attitude, and hiding in my room for a few hours.

Usually, this kind of frustration is directed toward my parents (or myself because I know they are right, but I am too proud to admit that, so I say that it is my parents), but it seems to always end up being directed at Lexy. You can imagine the strain that's put on our relationship. I know that the same thing happens with her, she's told me, but we always get frustrated either at each other, or at our parents together. We have often sat and talked about how annoying and frustrating our parents can be.

As I said, I am not excusing this behavior in any way. It is not a grown-up way to react when we (teenagers) don't get what we want. One big reason we react this way is pride. We do not want to admit that you were right and we were wrong, so we stick to our guns and just decide to get mad at the only people who could possibly be responsible—our parents. Also, we can be self-centered. These aren't just teenage problems, but human ones in general. We tend to think that whatever we want to do is more important than what anyone else has to do.

I mean, how would you prefer to spend your time, washing grimy dishes or watching your favorite television show? Tough choice? No, that is not a hard choice at all. However, certain things have to be done, and you understand that, as parents, you want your child to succeed. So you try to get us to do that certain job that you have told us to do one zillion times, and we get frustrated because you interrupted our favorite TV show at the climax. Then you get frustrated at us because you don't understand why we are frustrated with you. And the cycle continues.

Let me give you some advice. I'm not about to tell you to stop telling your kid what to do, but I will ask you to try to stop the cycle. When your kid or teen gets frustrated at you, put yourself into their skin for a minute. Think about when you were a teenager with crazy amounts of homework, who came home from school wanting to relax, whether it be before or after your homework. Think about how you felt when your parents told you to do the dishes or mow the lawn.

I am not saying to completely excuse this kind of behavior, especially if it happens all the time; however, don't make the situation worse by just yelling back at your kid. That only makes their pride kick in all the more, and that's when the problem starts getting really bad. So walk around in your teenager's skin a bit. Get a feel for how their life is because school is a full-time job, not to mention their actual job and all the social outings that they have to attend. Just remember, responding to frustration with frustration is like adding fuel to a fire. It only makes the problem worse.

15

Disappointed

Discipline Is Not "One Size Fits All"

I think the thing that took me the longest to understand was that in order to effectively discipline my children, I had to adjust my approach to what worked best for my very different girls. They are similar in their likes and their love for people, but their personalities are as different as night and day. I wouldn't say they are opposites, but they are close.

My oldest daughter has always been far easier to discipline than my youngest. For her, just knowing that I was disappointed in her was effective. Rarely did we have to resort to physical punishment or grounding. When we did, I think knowing we were upset almost outweighed the other punishment.

Our youngest is a different story entirely. There were times I would try and use the "dad is very disappointed" tone, and it seemed like she was saying, "So!" She wasn't, at least I don't think she was, but the approach was not nearly as effective with her as it was with her sister.

For the one, it brought about a desired change in behavior, but the other seemed to just take it and move forward without changing course at all. It was frustrating to say the least. I couldn't comprehend why such an effective technique worked with one and not the other. It was around this time in life that I began to understand what my dad meant when he would say, "Son, this hurts me worse than it hurts you."

I always thought, Oh yeah, let's trade places. I'll whip your backside this time, and we'll see who hurts more. Of course, I never said that out loud, but I thought it almost every time he said it. As I began to seek the most effective form of discipline for my youngest daughter, I began to realize it was so true. I hated seeing my girls sad or upset because they were being punished. It didn't matter if it was spanking or grounding them from their favorite things; I was hurt as much, if not more, because they eventually moved on to something else. But I still had the memory of the look they would give me while they were being punished.

It's not easy being a mom or a dad. It's hard to discipline your kids, and if it isn't, you probably need a little help. I have never felt joy because I was going to ground my child. I have never felt powerful or vindicated because of an "I told you so" moment. I have felt broken inside as my girls have had to learn hard lessons that I wish I could have helped them avoid, but it's part of the process.

Growing up is hard too. Discipline is necessary. Correction is one of the most important things we as parents do. It's a huge responsibility, and if we neglect that because we want our kids to like us, we are doing more harm than good. We cripple our kids when we don't teach them principles of responsibility or allow them to reap the consequences of what they've sown. Sometimes we have to correct verbally, but other times require a tougher approach. I have had to spank my kids. I've had to tell them they couldn't do something they really wanted to do as a result of their behavior. I've seen them cry and wanted so much to give in and say, "Never mind, you can go," but what would that accomplish?

Honestly, what the Bible refers to when it says "Spare the rod, spoil the child" has been proven many times in our society. Spend a little time at any of your local stores, and I'm sure you'll encounter a youngster who's been a little spoiled! Our responsibility as parents isn't to lord over our children; it's to train them so that some day they can have something to fall back on when they have kids of their own. If we train them while they're young, they won't forget it when they're old!

Discipline has to be motivated at the center by love. Without love, the discipline we give is as ineffective as fighting a fire with a water balloon. Effective discipline requires a solid relationship, which requires time to build. Love is what helps us stand firm, when inside we are crushed because we've hurt this little person whom we would die for if we had to. Discipline without love destroys. Discipline with love builds and strengthens the one being corrected! As much as I despise saying things my parents said to me, it truly does hurt me more than it hurts them, but I know that it's necessary. In the end, it's those moments that bring joy to our hearts as parents as we look at where they had been, compared to where they are now. Being a dad has helped me to understand my heavenly Father more than anything else. I understand the lengths a father will go for the children he loves. I am so thankful for the opportunity to be a dad! It's changed my life.

Discipline isn't pleasant, but it's necessary. Someday your child will be there in your shoes, and in that moment, they will understand. Don't avoid it because it hurts. Love requires discipline to be fully realized. I know there have been moments in my life where my parents had to let me learn things the hard way or punish me because I had done something wrong, and I'm thankful that they loved me enough to do what was necessary so that I could become who I am today. I didn't understand it at the time, but I do now, and your kids will too! Understand it will take time, and it requires relationship so that you can discipline in the most effective way for each of your children. It might be easier if it were, but it isn't, "one style fits all"!

Bria

Different people discipline their kids in different ways. Some parents are harsh and use physical discipline over verbal, and vice versa. Sometimes, harsh discipline can push kids away and make them rebellious. Other parents, afraid to upset their children, hardly discipline their children at all. This often leads to selfish children who are used to getting whatever they want and causes attitude problems that completely counteract the parents' intentions.

With new technology, movies, and societal views, it can be incredibly difficult to find a good balance of discipline in today's society. Technology distracts people and makes them even more impatient than before. Movies tend to portray parents as villains, desperate to destroy their children's happiness. Society, many times as a result of the way media portrays parents, sees a parent who strictly disciplines their child as cruel.

What happens a lot of times is people want parents to be friends with their kids, and that just isn't the way it's supposed to be. Parents are teachers. They are here to help their children grow, which often means disciplining them. If a teacher and student become friends before the teaching process is over, that can taint the relationship and make the teacher not do their job properly. It is the same with parents. One day, after children grow up, the relationship can and, often should, evolve to become a friendship.

Now I am not saying that parents should just be cruel and mean to their children, and I am not saying that children are the only ones who learn from the parent-child relationship. Being a parent is as much a learning experience as being a child is. Also, parents should be reasonable and try to understand their position. But there are many times when discipline is important. Without discipline, a person cannot grow.

It is hard for a tree to grow in a rain forest. The canopy makes it hard to reach the sun, and the harsh elements make it hard for the roots to hold on, but through hardwork, a tree will grow to staggering heights. However, it has to go through all the hard stuff before it can become a giant. This is similar to discipline. If persons do not have discipline in their life, they will not be able to function when they have to fend for themselves.

The most important thing in this chapter is to not set discipline aside in an effort to be friends with your child. However, a close second would be finding balance, and more specifically, deciding what form of discipline to use. When people think of discipline, they usually think of physical discipline, such as spanking. Another common form would be grounding, the punitive confiscation of stuff. These two specifically are what most of society thinks of when they think of discipline, and consequently, they are the ones that are most featured in movies and TV. While these forms of discipline do exist and are sometimes necessary, there is another form of discipline that works very well, especially if a good parent-child relationship has been established. That is verbal correction.

It seems apparent to me that many parents in today's society underestimate the power of the word disappointed.

Children look up to their parents and want them to be pleased with them and their work. You have to look no further than a child running to their mom or dad with a scribbled picture saying, "Look what I did!" to see the truth in this statement. When a child hears their parent tell them that they are disappointed in them, something happens in their little minds that can be hard to explain. Being told that their parent is disappointed in them is almost like being rejected, but it isn't all bad. If executed correctly, verbal correction can be the most effective form of discipline there is. It makes a child want to try harder to avoid that feeling and to not let their parent down. It's kind of like if your hero came up to you and told you he or she was disappointed in you. How would that make you feel? Verbal correction has a similar effect on children.

Also, verbal correction isn't just for little kids, it's for teenagers too. Again, think about your personal hero telling you that he or she was disappointed in you. If it would make both an adult and a child feel upset, why would it not make a teenager feel the same? Telling a teenager that you are disappointed in them will have an effect similar to that which a child feels when the same thing is said to them. I know that if my dad tells me that he is disappointed in me, it makes me immediately want to do better. The effect is slightly different though. With a child, it is just that they do not want to let their parents down, and that is a factor with teenagers; however, for a teenager it can very much be a matter of pride. If a teenager is told that someone is disappointed in them, especially someone they look up to, they see it as though they did something wrong, and then their pride kicks in. They want whatever they do to be right. So the word disappointed has a very similar effect on both little kids and teenagers, though it may be slightly different.

Discipline is one of the most important parts of parenting. There are several kinds of discipline, but often the most effective form is verbal correction. Do not yell at a child harshly that they are wrong all the time because that has the same effect that over-the-top physical discipline has. The word disappointed bears a huge weight in the minds of children and teenagers; don't be afraid to use it. Now there are times when grounding or spanking is appropriate. In those times, do not be afraid to discipline your child accordingly. They may not be entirely happy with you, or you with yourself in the moment, but it will all be worth it when your child finally grows to reach the light.

16

Asking the Hard Questions

No parent ever wants to think that their child is lying to them. Especially in the church world, we like to imagine that all the pressures the world brings to bear impact others, but not our kids. After all, they were raised in church. They know I love them! They'd never hide anything from me!

We have a lot of excuses as parents to explain our avoidance of the tough conversations that life requires. We are shocked when we discover that our children are struggling with the same things the "worldly" kids struggle with. It's safe to say that most kids, churched or unchurched, have at some point, thought about suicide. The teen sitting in a pew is just as likely to have confidence issues, struggle with lust, or use recreational drugs. Sometimes I think they are more likely to go down that path.

We insulate our kids from the difficult things in life, hoping it will help them make wise choices when confronted with a situation in which their integrity and values come under attack. In reality, we disarm them. We set our kids up for a fall, all in an attempt to protect them from the world. They feel cheated, like we were lying to them. Is it any wonder cutting, alcohol abuse, teen pregnancy, and homosexuality are as common in churched youth as in the unchurched?

We approach the topics with a naivety that opens the door to irresponsibility as parents, as though avoiding the discussions would make them magically disappear from the life of our kids. I know it's uncomfortable, but we need to talk to our kids about sex, about the changes their bodies are going through, about depression, and every other topic we don't want to discuss because we assume a Christian upbringing makes them immune to the temptations the world presents. If we never talk to them about drugs or sex, they'll figure it out for themselves, and if they can't figure it out, the world is more than happy to fill in the blanks.

We naively believe that our children will come to us if they are struggling because we're good Christian parents, but that is the exact reason that they won't. Your child isn't going to initiate the difficult conversations that need to be had; that's our job. Parenting isn't easy, but neither is being a teenager in a world that tries to glorify all of the things that can destroy them if they aren't prepared to deal with them. Love isn't burying our head in the sand, hoping that our kids will follow suit. Love is patiently sitting with your children and asking them the hard questions and being prepared to hear the answers we hope to never hear, and loving them no matter what.

Kids are kids, whether they are raised in a Christian home or in the home of an atheist. They will face the same temptations. If we think avoiding topics will prepare our kids for the tough choices this life has for them, then we are only fooling ourselves. As uncomfortable as it may be to discuss the topics of suicide, sex, and drug abuse with my kids, I have to do it. It has to be done in an open forum where there isn't fear of punishment or else they won't be honest—and honesty is the best tool we have to address those messy subjects.

I'm not suggesting that you sit down and tell your four–year-old all that you know about sex, but if you wait until that child is thirteen, you've missed your window to be a positive influence in your child's life. Be assured that the kids on the bus are talking about it, and not only in high school, but in elementary school as well. I was first approached to try drugs when I was in the second grade. I didn't, but not because my parents told me about the dangers of drug use, I just wasn't interested. I can tell you for a fact, there are elementary school kids out there who drink and use drugs.

According to a survey conducted by the Partnership for a Drug-Free America in 1999 known as PATS (Partnership Attitude Tracking Study) that sampled two thousand, three hundred students in one hundred and fifty schools indicated that from fourth through sixth grade, alcohol consumption nearly tripled within the sample. The survey concludes that 9.8% of fourth graders had tried more than a sip of alcohol in the previous year with an alarming 29.4% of sixth graders making the same claim over the same time period. According to the survey, racial differences had very little to do with the numbers, though boys were much more likely than girls to drink at a ratio of two to one. A more recent report by the CDC citing two surveys, one from 2012 and another from 2013, shows things haven't declined, adolescent and teen drinking is increasing.

Other surveys indicate the preferred alcoholic beverages of elementary students are beer and wine. The PRIDE Survey conducted in 2001-2002 included approximately 25,000 students and concluded that approximately 11% of the students who admitted to drinking would drink from one to seven times per week. And those numbers are only the students who admitted to using or trying alcohol! These are elementary school students and that number is shockingly high.

Those same kids attend the same schools your kids do. Whose opinion do you want shaping your child's decision-making, yours, or a second grader whose parents openly abuse drugs in front of them? We can kid ourselves and say it isn't happening, but don't be surprised when you find yourself having to have much harder conversations later in life because it was just easier to believe it would never happen to your kids.

Too many times, Christian parents find themselves shocked by what their kids have gotten into. We live in a bubble and rarely realize that the world is clamoring to get in. Most churched families have few unchurched relationships outside of their own extended families. Most of those are so caught up with the day-to-day life of the American family, from school to church to sports, it's hard to find time to be together, let alone expand our circle of influence. We become isolated. Because we are so busy doing the things that consume our day-to-day lives, we sometimes overlook the signs that the kids are showing us. We figure we will get to having those necessary discussions some other day because we're too tired, or we just don't feel like fighting that fight at the moment.

The problem is we're probably never really going to feel like dealing with the issues of today's society. Our kids are more than happy to avoid the topics. Somewhere, somehow we have to make the uncomfortable choices. Yes, it may be embarrassing for you, and almost definitely embarrassing for your child, but better to have honest discussion about life's difficult choices than too assume there aren't any issues in their lives.

I think one reason we avoid the topics that need to be addressed is because, inside, we're afraid what their answers might reveal about us as parents. We're afraid for them, but not enough to face the potential truth that our child struggles with something we never imagined they would deal with. So, out of selfishness, we avoid discussing those things because we want to believe that we are great parents.

We are more concerned with how our child's poor decisions reflect on us as parents than how we can help them grow and overcome areas of weakness in their lives. We turn a blind eye to the signs to avoid the painful reality that we don't know everything about our kids, and that we aren't quite as cool in their eyes as we hoped to be.

We strive for friendships, but the young people of this world need role models. They need parents who are less concerned with appearing cool to their child's friends and more concerned with what their kid's are seeing, hearing, and feeling when they aren't with us. Your kids won't always think you're cool, and honestly, they couldn't care less if their friends think you are. In fact, your behavior probably irritates them. A child needs a parent to care enough to confront the difficult issues that they have to deal with every day. They don't need you to judge them. They need you to walk through this life beside them, helping them up when they fall, and sharing the wisdom you've gained through your own experiences. Be vulnerable with each other. Cry with each other. Show your child that when they are hurt, you are hurt. Bear their burdens with them. Look for answers together.

The only way any of that is possible is through healthy communication between you and your child. You can't be their friend, but you can develop a relationship that will lead to friendship one day! Be a parent first; friendship comes after the obstacles of adolescence are overcome!

Bria

There are many pressing problems in America today. There are many temptations that teenagers face every day. Teen years are a time of fun and exploration, and sadly, sometimes the temptation is too much. We cannot ignore these issues. Problems like drugs, alcohol, tobacco, self-harm, depression, and suicide are very real, and catalysts for these problems fill a teenager's life. Parents, you need to sit down with your kid or kids and talk to them about these things.

One thing you need to make sure you do is always try to make sure they are doing okay and know your child well enough to know when they are lying to you. If you know they are lying to you, don't let them keep lying. Keep asking them until you get the truth and don't be afraid to go to their teachers and counselors. If your child is not homeschooled, then their teachers see them almost as often as you do, and they see your child in a different environment than you typically do.

Make sure you sit down with your kid or kids and discuss these hard topics with them. Don't wait for them to bring it up to you. A teenager is not going to initiate that conversation, so the job falls to you as a parent to cross that gap. These conversations can be awkward, and your child may not seem to appreciate it when you start the conversation; however, they will thank you later. A lot of kids get into bad situations simply because no one took the time to make sure they were out of them.

During these conversations, make sure that they know that you still love them no matter what they tell you. Manage your tone so that they don't feel threatened, but still know that you are absolutely serious. You love your child, and you want to make sure that they are safe and not doing anything that could get them into serious trouble. If your child feels threatened, they will shut down and may not tell you the truth. Start having these talks with your child quite early. I would say as early as nine or ten years old. Having these tough conversations relatively frequently will help keep your child from ever getting into these sorts of things and feeling like they need to lie to you. If your child is already past this age and into his or her teenage years, don't think that it's too late to start. It may be slightly harder for you to get the conversation going, but these conversations will be one of the best things you can do for your child and for yourself as a parent.

I have seen the positive results of having such conversations not just in my own life, but in the lives of others at my school. For example, I was helping do some interviews for new applicants for a club at my school, and one girl's interview was outstanding. One of the things that specifically stood out was the fact that she mentioned having frequent conversations with her mom about various things. Whether it was something as trivial as the daily happenings at school or a serious topic like drugs and alcohol, she and her mother would have daily conversations, and these conversations have influenced her life in a positive way. The same can be said for the conversations my dad or mom and I have. My perspective on many things would be completely different if my parents had not been sure to discuss serious topics with me.

Also, these conversations and the manner in which they were handled increase my faith in the fact that I can come to my parents with anything, like if I was at a party and there were drugs and alcohol that I did not expect to be there. I know that I could call my mom or my dad and ask them to come pick me up and not be scared that they would be misunderstanding. Also, I feel like my honesty in those conversations has boosted my parents' confidence in my integrity so that they may not have to worry quite as much about the choices I am faced with daily.

Problems like drugs, alcohol, tobacco, and depression cannot be combatted solely in a classroom. We as teenagers are looking to you as parents, whether we realize it or not, to become involved in our lives and ask us hard questions. If you don't ask these questions and show us that you care and that these things are bad, we will look to other adults in our life, such as celebrities. Start asking these hard questions and stop your child from getting the wrong impression on these issues. They may not be entirely joyful when you start to ask them if anyone has offered them drugs, but in the long run, it will benefit both you and your child.

17

Two Girls, Twice the Headaches

When our second daughter arrived three years after our oldest, it created an interesting dynamic for me. I was working part-time on a volunteer basis for a local church and part-time for a local sign company. Our neighbor would watch our oldest when the sign shop needed me. It was an awesome arrangement. I would work for three to four hours, typically around nap time, and our neighbor worked as a crossing guard so she was home and available during that time.

I thought everything was under control. Then our youngest was born, and my balance was off. It was more difficult to leave with the new baby at the house. I had to divide my time between both, and since we had a newborn, my oldest typically got the short end of the deal. She had been used to having me all to herself, and then this new baby began to infringe upon her time with Daddy.

In all honesty, I don't remember the transition being as hard for our oldest as it was for me. I guess I felt guilty because sometimes I couldn't play with her since I was holding the baby or feeding the baby. I don't know how families that have twins and triplets do it. I had one diaper to change and one child potty training. They have two or three, and I'm pretty sure they conspire to go at the same time. I know ours did.

I can remember moments when our oldest would be yelling, "Dad, I'm done!" while I was changing yet another smelly diaper. The challenge of changing one child is bad enough with all the wiggling and rolling. Add to that the fear that your toilet-training child is going to suddenly decide to jump down from the toilet and run into the living room to watch cartoons, or worse yet, wipe herself!

I managed to get through the sticky moments and even figured out ways to get the oldest involved in the process, so we were still spending time together. I'd let her help feed her sister. Sweet moments when she was helping with the bottle; not so sweet when it was baby food. Still, I would take advantage of the moments that presented themselves each day. When the baby was sleeping and her sister wasn't, we would read, play a game or watch one of her favorite shows. When they were both sleeping, sometimes I would nap or, if the neighbor was available, I'd run over and put a couple of hours in at the sign shop. We managed. Sometimes I was completely exhausted and felt like a contortionist, but it worked, and it was worth it.

Building memories from the earliest days of a child's life becomes the blocks that relationship is built upon as they grow. The silly little things, like letting them put every barrette and hair clip they could find in my hair, or pretending that they had broken my arm or leg while they ran over to doctor me, those moments are the glue that holds things together. I'm a firm believer that, regardless of whether you have boys, girls, or both, time is the most valuable thing you can give them.

Don't ever make them feel like they are an obstacle to you achieving some goal, or that spending time with them is keeping you from something you'd rather be doing. That's a hard thing to do because a lot of times, there are things we need to be doing as dads and parents, but if you don't, you're pulling at the foundation. If you've ever made a tower out of Legos, you know that it's far quicker to destroy what's been built than to build it.

The sacrifice is worth it. When you make the moments you have count, then the times when you can't stop and play are much easier to overcome. There will be moments when your child's expectations won't be met, and that's okay. Make sure those moments don't outweigh the moments when their expectations are met.

Especially with girls, those moments will be a foundational principle that will guide them through the rest of their lives. Relationships will be measured against them. Make them count. There are far too many young ladies out there who, during their formative years, their fathers weren't there or didn't make the most of the opportunities they had together. Those young ladies seek love and acceptance through relationships that don't have solid foundation because they don't have anything to fall back on. They turn to the first guy who shows an interest and typically it ends poorly. A cycle of bad relationships begins and continues to spiral further and further down.

So many dads wonder what their children are thinking. They frantically try to reestablish relationship at a time when the lines of communication aren't very strong. They wring their hands in frustration because they can't seem to get through. Simply put, they have no investment to draw from. There isn't any emotional capital to get them through those moments because the investment wasn't made when it needed to be.

The value of time spent during the first five to ten years of life can't be replaced. Gifts can't build a solid foundation, in fact, they build unrealistic expectations in the life of a child who needs you. Your time is the key and can't be compensated by anything. Trying to build a strong relationship with a child after the age of ten is difficult. It will cost you something to create the trust that is necessary to make a significant impact if you start the process late. By all means, start now if you haven't. But if your kids are still in that impressionable time of life, make the investment and make it count!

Bria

I really don't remember what it was like to be an only child. I was only three when Lexy was born, so I didn't really retain many memories of my life before her. However, I do have friends who are the only child in their families, and sometimes I compare my life to theirs. It's strange for me to see a bathroom that is only set up for one person, or to see only one bedroom meant for one kid in a house. The life of an only child is often alien to me. Sometimes, my sister will stay at someone else's house for a day or two, and I will get a small taste of what it is like to be an only child. There isn't anyone fighting me for a spot on the couch or that last little bit of room at the bathroom counter.

Having a sister isn't all fun and games. People say that girls are made of "sugar and spice and everything nice," but there is just something about girls in general that is not so sweet. Many times, sisters are the ones who see that side of each other more than anyone else, especially in my house. I am not saying that my sister and I are always perfect angels in public, but we can be the farthest from angels at home. We get irritated with each other over something small, like someone getting ready on the wrong side of the counter, or using the other's perfume without expressly asking first. We get irritated outside the house and in the house, and because we are so close, a lot of times that anger gets taken out on each other.

It is a lot harder to do things like getting ready in the morning when you have a sister. After a while, a pattern forms, but that pattern is always broken at some point. For example, my sister and I have had plenty of time to form a pattern for getting ready in the mornings. One unspoken rule that almost never changes is that Lexy does her makeup and hair and everything on the right hand side of the counter, and I do everything on the left. It just works. However, sometimes I will walk into the bathroom to take a shower, and Lexy is already in there getting ready, on the left side of the counter. It's not the end of the world, but it makes things a little bit harder for me to take a shower and get ready when she stands there because of the way our bathroom is set up. Other than just standing on the correct side of the bathroom counter, things like having to move around in different rooms and getting in each other's way more often than not are things that are inescapable in a sister relationship. Part of me is just glad that I only have one sister. Once a year, my sister and I spend a week at a family from the church's house. They have two girls. It is hard enough to handle four teen girls in one house for one week out of the year. I can't imagine having to work around that many people year-round.

Having two girls in the house is an adventure. Just getting ready in the morning can feel like a quest because there is someone else there in the way. Being an only child can feel appealing on occasion. I mean, you don't have to worry about fighting your way to the sink or arguing over stupid little things nearly as much. But even in those times when being an only child looks great, I would never trade anything in my life to become one. My sister is my absolute best friend. What I said earlier in this chapter about us seeing the worst in each other is true; however, many times we not only get to see it, but we bring out the best in each other. She may give me headaches sometimes, and I'm sure that I give her some too. But I am who I am today because of Lexy, and I would never give up that relationship, even if she does dance on every single remaining nerve from time to time.

18

Ready…Fight!

I don't know if I will ever understand why two people who have so much in common fight *so* much! I wasn't fortunate enough to have a sibling close to my own age, so by the time my little sister Jennifer came along, I was eleven years old. I felt more of a responsibility to help her grow up more than anything. I know competition for mom and dad's attention has a lot to do with it, but I still don't get it.

When my brother and sister were little, they got along, but there came a point where I began to wonder if one might smother the other in their sleep. Now I'm seeing very similar behavior in my girls. They talk to each other in the most awful tone and say things that I know are meant to hurt the other as deeply as possible. I have thought I was losing my mind and at times, I think I definitely have.

It's amazing how quickly situations escalate. They can be smiling and laughing, seemingly enjoying each others company, then, without warning, one is mad at the other and making weird facial expressions as they shout their frustration in an angry voice. Sometimes it's a result of one or the other taking something too far, like wrestling/tickling or flinging their arms about as they dance around. Other times, it's because one of them doesn't like the way the other is doing some activity, and they want to offer advice.

Often though, my oldest, being far more mature due to her additional three years of life, feels compelled to take a maternal role with her sister. This never goes as well as our oldest hopes it will. Can you imagine your younger sister not wanting to take advantage of the vast amounts of knowledge those three years have given her? It's ironic because the same child looks at her mother and I as though we've lost our minds and couldn't possibly have anything of value to offer her through our experience.

I had that moment in my life where I looked at the things my mom and dad had told me, and I realized that much, if not most of it, was right. I understand the desire to grow up and find one's own footing, to have the respect that one so deeply desires. Everyone wants to feel respected, that they have something special to offer. People want others to look up to them and depend on them, especially those that they love. I can see how that might lead to conflict, but I don't understand it. It doesn't make sense!

My youngest child wants her older sister to respect her and believe in her. My oldest wants her younger sister to do the same thing. They both want to feel like they have something of value to offer the relationship. They want the other to know that they have their best interest at heart. So why do those two get so irritated with each other so easily?

That same desire one has to have their opinion respected is the driving force behind the other getting irritated because they feel the other doesn't respect them. It's a vicious circle! Sometimes I think it would be far easier to let them fight it out, but I don't think that's the healthiest of solutions. There is a time to let them resolve their own conflict, but we should always be there, ready to offer advice, and to restrain, if necessary.

If they never figure out how to resolve conflicts in a healthy manner, they will struggle throughout their lives. Though the fights they get in push me to the edge, and sometimes beyond, I can't always swoop in and stop them from handling the situation themselves. Conflict resolution is hardest when those we are in conflict with are close to our hearts. It's preparation for later in life. Our job as parents is to teach them and guide them as they discover how to resolve disputes in an effective manner. It's also a great opportunity to teach them the value of forgiveness and the power of apology. It's stressful for us, but essential for their development. As long as no one gets physically hurt, it's okay to let them deal with it. But you might want to buy a ref's uniform. Sometimes you feel more like a referee than a parent!

Bria

My little sister Lexy, in many ways, is my best friend, even if sometimes she does feel like a nemesis. Don't get me wrong. I love her so much, but there are times (sometimes frequent) that she just gets on my nerves. There are the times I get annoyed for the silliest little thing, and then there are times when she insists on antagonizing me until I just want to rip my hair out. When I think about it though, I see that she is like me, and I'm like her. We definitely have our differences, but if I dig down past the obvious, I see that she has picked up many things from me over the years, and vice versa.

Many of my best memories are of times I spent with my sister—times like singing Disney songs at the top of our lungs and dancing to them shamelessly. Others include riding rides and screaming at Disney World, countless road trips, or using leftover fireworks the day after Fourth of July to blow up old stuffed animals. Some of the best, most thought-provoking conversations are among those I have had with Lexy. We laugh, sing, talk, and dance together. However, we don't always get along like we do at those times. We yell at each other or shut each other out. But sometimes, some of our best conversations come out of those times, and I discover things about her, she discovers things about me, and even I discover things I didn't know about myself. Yeah, we may fight quite a bit, but our bond is strong enough to last through the tough times and even becomes stronger through them.

I love Lexy with all my heart, but there are times I forget to show it. I wish that I could write that Lexy and I always get along and are always doing things together, but that would be a lie. There is still a long way to go before I am the perfect big sister, but I still am working at it.

Now we don't always get along, but that doesn't mean we are always fighting either. Lexy and I love to play games, watch movies, dance, and just sit together. We like to shoot each other with Nerf guns. We cook, clean, and work together. We fight, but those disputes can never overcome the fun we have together and the love we have for each other.

There is a verse in the Bible that says that God is a friend who sticks closer than a brother. The term brother could be changed out for sister any time. As I previously stated, Lexy is my best friend. I cannot imagine my life without her because she has always been there. If someone were to ask me to describe the sister relationship, I would say that a sister is a friend who is always by your side, even when you don't want her to be. Part of the reason might be because you live in the same house, and you can't get away from each other, but there is something more to it. It isn't just that you can't get away from each other; it's that you want to be there to help them and guide them. You could also use the expression "two sides of the same coin." Sisters are very different. But very early on, there comes a point when you realize that the two (or more) are in many ways of the same mind. For example, there are many times when Lexy will start to make a reference and get as far as, "I loved it when…" and then forget what she was trying to say. Many of those times, it takes me all of two seconds to finish the reference. Lexy and I like a lot of the same stuff and share many opinions, and when we disagree, we may butt heads for a while, but we don't let it come between us.

One of the main things that makes Lexy my best friend is that we know we can tell each other anything. I know that I can tell her anything that's going on, and she will listen. She knows the same about me. In fact, I think there are a few conversations we've had that nobody but the two of us know about. They will stay that way until I have her permission to share them. There are plenty of highs and lows, and I will gladly go through the lows to get the highs every time because they are worth it.

Being a big sister is tough. You're expected to set an example for your younger sibling (or siblings) and help them. That can be hard to do when you feel annoyed toward them all the time. Sometimes you have to be the bigger person and just deal with the upsets the best you can to make the relationship the best you can. Sometimes you have to be an ear to talk to, a shoulder to cry on, or a target to shoot with a foam dart. All those things are good to be. Another trick is trusting your sibling enough to return the favor.

Being a big sister has meant a lot to me. My sister is my best friend. She has been able to teach me things that can't be learned from a book or an adult. She has always been there for me, and I try to be there for her. Being there for someone is complicated to explain. Truly always being there is being ready to be anything another person needs, whether that is a shoulder to cry on, a person to yell at, or a friend to laugh with. Being there for someone is one of the truest synonyms for love that there is. To be there for someone means to be willing to lay down what is important to you for what is important to them. My sister and I are still working on our relationship, but we love each other. No fight or argument will ever make either one of us love the other any less than we do now. We may not like each other all the time, but the love we share is too strong to be uprooted by a fight or an argument.

19

Mr. Fix-It

I love teaching my girls how to fix things! From meals to an oil change, they need to know how to take care of things because someday they might need to do those things on their own. A young lady should be just as comfortable holding a hammer as a makeup brush! Hopefully, she will find herself in a marriage one day where she won't have to use those skills. But I'd rather them know how to do something if they need to do it.

We are too quick to say that an ability should be based on one's gender. A girl, knowing how to use a screwdriver for its intended purpose, rather than as a punch to add an extra notch in a belt, is a good thing for the young lady and the screwdriver! Just because she's a girl, she shouldn't be put into a helpless situation because she gets a flat, anymore than a young man should be clueless in the kitchen or the laundry room. Some skills are valuable regardless of gender.

One of my favorite memories with my youngest daughter happened when she helped me change a part on her mother's car. I even let her turn a wrench a time or two. I wasn't trying to be mean! Some of the best teaching opportunities come when we find ourselves in a working environment. Good conversations happen and positive reinforcement comes as you praise them for doing a job well done. There's something disarming about holding a tool in your hands and working side by side with someone. You build trust as you teach them how to do something as simple as painting a fence or raking a yard.

Building things together can do more to strengthen your relationship with your child than hours spent watching them from the stands at a sporting event. Both are important, but there's something about sweating together that breaks down barriers and leads to meaningful conversations, which never would have happened while we cheer from the sidelines. Engaging them and connecting with them in a more direct manner creates a bond that isn't easily broken.

We make it fun, don't get me wrong. We sing songs and talk about ridiculous stuff sometimes, but we make the most of the opportunity. There's nothing like raking the yard into an immense pile of leaves, then jumping in, sinking past your head. It's a lot of work, but it teaches them to value what they've accomplished.

We tend to appreciate the things we have to work for more than the things that are given to us. When they are a part of the process, whether preparing a meal or building a swing set, they get more out of it! There is pride in knowing that they had a hand in creating, and it helps them to understand your love for them a little bit more. They will appreciate what you do together more than anything you just hand to them. It's an added benefit to what they've learned.

Don't assume that your daughter doesn't have an interest in something because she's a girl. The same goes for your son! Teach them everything you know so that someday they can pass on what they've learned to your grandkids. They will appreciate that you were willing to take the time to teach them when they find themselves in an awkward situation, which they could overcome because of some lesson you taught them.

A girl changing a tire on the side of the road isn't an ideal situation, but it's better than her being stranded without cell phone service, hoping that the person who passes her by will be compassionate enough to help, or that they are safe and won't harm her. Teach them how so that they don't have to feel helpless. It empowers them and helps them to realize that they can do anything if they put their mind to it!

I wish I could fix the issues they deal with in the same way. Being a man, I want to fix the problems they face. In many ways, building a house is easier than raising a child. It's predictable! When something doesn't work, it can be fixed or replaced. The pieces can be brought together if we understand how they fit. If a car makes a grinding noise when you stop, you know you need to change the brake pads, so you do and it's better. When your daughter cries for no reason, or goes from happy to hate in a matter of seconds, you want to identify the problem; buy a new part and fix it—but it doesn't work that way. If it were only that easy!

We have to have a different set of tools for working on those problems. A shoulder for crying on and an ear to hear are a good start, but it's also important to be able to avoid the natural impulse to fix the situation. Some things will fix themselves only when we don't try to fix it for them. It's hard because when those we care about are hurt, we want to pick up a sword and fight whatever is causing the pain. That's a good thing! We need to be the knight, and they need to know we're willing. But they also need to learn to fight those things and fix what's wrong on their own. It empowers them, just like teaching them to change their own tire. Apparently, there are some things duct tape won't fix!

Bria

Sometimes, I make myself and everyone around me laugh because I have trouble leaving something broken. I have a specific friend who knows this and takes advantage of it, when she has something like a necklace tangled up. It's like a puzzle that I have to solve. If something breaks, I like to try to put it back together. Things like dolls, doors, lights, and jewelry just cannot be left broken in my mind. For example, I had this pair of earrings that I adored, but one of them broke. I spent the next half hour studying the unbroken earring so that I could fix the broken one.

I get this drive to fix things from my dad. Ever since I was little, he has been showing my sister and me how to fix things. I have helped change out a radiator, take out a garden tractor starter, and replace a car battery and battery cables that were not designed in the most convenient way. My dad just likes to show us how to fix things, and as a result of that, if something is broken around me, I am not able to move on without fixing it.

My dad has always recruited my sister and me to help on various projects. We have experience in everything, from simple car repairs to painting to removing carpet and putting in hardwood. We often get our hands dirty and put things together or tear them apart. All too often, fathers will teach their sons how to fix things, but they don't try to teach these things to their daughters. Don't just think that because she is a little girl, she can't or won't want to fix things with you. That couldn't be farther from the truth.

One of the main things that made fixing things so special when I was little was that it gave me another connection with my dad. I guess it just made me feel important. Fixing cars was my dad's thing, and every so often, he would ask me to help him. It made me feel needed and a little bit grown-up.

There aren't just literal, physical things that a father and daughter need to fix together. There are plenty of emotional problems that a father should work out with his daughter. Don't let her shut you out. If something is wrong, try to figure it out and find out what you can do to help her get through it. And don't forget to let her do the same. Don't try to handle all of your problems on your own. The support system of the father-daughter relationship goes both ways.

Now there isn't some panacea or all-purpose tool to fix issues in life. Oftentimes, every struggle in life has to be treated as an isolated incident. It isn't bad to refer to past events to try to find a solution to the issue, but don't be surprised if it isn't the exact thing she needs at that precise moment. Sometimes she will need a joke to make her laugh, other times a voice of advice, other times a shoulder to cry on, and still other times just an ear to listen to her.

Sometimes, fixing a broken heart is the hardest job there is, but it is an important responsibility of a father to be there to help his little girl through those tough times, no matter how challenging and frustrating these are. I know that many times you just want to be able to look inside her heart and fix whatever is broken, but it's not that simple. I know it can be frustrating when you look at a problem and just don't see a way to fix it. Just be patient and listen—pray. Do what you can to figure out what you can do for her. Sometimes, the fix is simple, but other times it takes a bit more work.

20

And They Let Me Use Explosives!

Since I was a kid, I have had a fascination for fireworks. I have a lot of memories that involve them. From Pops to mortar shells and everything in between, I love fireworks! I would go so far as to say that my favorite holiday is the Fourth of July. I know, Christmas is a pretty big deal, but lighting a pack of firecrackers doesn't really work on December 25th.

My children have adopted my love for those wonderful noisemakers. It's really probably not a good thing! My oldest remembers the day I blew up a Barbie house, or the time I filled a stuffed animal with enough fireworks to blow the head off, as fondly as trips to Disney World or Christmas morning. Some of you reading this right now have probably began to question my sanity, but I don't care.

From the time they were old enough to hold a sparkler without lighting each other on fire, my girls have been a part of the memories. As they've gotten older, I've let them help me choose what we're buying on our annual trip to the old store we've bought from for the past several years. The store is so old and dusty that you kind of worry that a stray bit of static might send the whole place up but it would be spectacular to watch.

I'm not sure why I have such a fondness for explosions. I don't typically like blowing things up. I've never made bombs or intentionally started something on fire that shouldn't have been burnt. I remember as a kid how excited I would be when the Fourth rolled around. Sometimes, my dad would smuggle me a pack or two of firecrackers because when I was growing up, they were illegal in Michigan. We would go to the local park and watch the big show, and I was mesmerized.

I even like the little snakes that grow when you light the little tablet. My mom and stepdad would bring those home, and I couldn't wait to light them and watch them grow. In that moment, everything seemed to make sense. Maybe it was a release for all the pent-up frustrations I had growing up, watching my parents fighting. I felt like I was stuck in the middle. Sometimes I wanted to explode! There was something relaxing about watching those blooms of colored sparks, flying through the air. Something so beautiful couldn't be bad!

I'm glad my daughters and I have formed new fond memories of our times spent blowing stuff up. I've seen a number of students in youth ministry whom I have shared a lot of those memories with. From blowing up dollhouses to our impromptu fireworks shows behind the church when it was raining and no one wanted to watch, we had the time of our lives. Something so simple can bring so much joy. It feels like a celebration every time one goes off.

I think it's the predictability. You light the wick, it ignites the powder and—boom!—let the fun commence. I always have felt a little rebellious, and when my dad would bring those contraband fireworks, it made me smile. I knew that he cared about me because he knew how much I loved to set them off. He gave them to me even though I probably shouldn't have had them. As ridiculous as it may sound, it was at those times when I was growing up that I felt closest to my dad. Fortunately, no one ever got injured or fined.

I think those memories are one of the reasons I continue to love fireworks to this day. It isn't really about the explosions; it's about the time spent together, anticipating what's coming. Lighting that wick, running for cover, and staring up at the sky together, waiting for the magical burst of color to fill the air—that's what it's all about. I can't wait until next year! Fortunately, it's legal to shoot them off where I live!

Bria

Another set of memories that I have with my dad revolve around Fourth of July. My dad and I have bonded over countless explosions. Every year, we go to a little fireworks place and get like three big bags full of fireworks. My dad used to be in charge of the fireworks show for the church, but now we can only really do small stuff up by the road or in the driveway. Still, we have so much fun! There's just something about exploding, colorful sparks, and loud booms that just excites my family.

I specifically remember one Independence Day a few years ago. We were having a party at our church and it rained. However, that did not stop my dad and a group of men from the church on their quest to obliterate my best friend's old dollhouse. They weren't being mean or anything. The dollhouse had been donated to the nursery a year or two before, and no one really used it anymore.

Drawn to the sights and sounds of the explosions, my sister, my best friend, and I ran to the small storage room that had glass doors and offered a sufficient view of the destruction from a safe distance. It was glorious! Sparks and water flew with every explosion. As a final act, my dad had twisted the wicks of six mortar shells together and put them on the top floor of the two-story dollhouse. It is safe to say that was one of the loudest moments of my life. When my dad and his friends decided that had been enough, the roof of the house was a blackish green. It was amazing!

The following day, my dad got together a group of people from the church to finish off the remaining fireworks, and my sister and I were among them. There was a war (which I am in no way advocating; throwing explosives at people is dangerous). Someone lit a smoke bomb in my dad's office, which made it smell for hours, possibly days. But the pinnacle of this day was the stuffed animals.

In a back closet in the church, we made an amazing discovery. There was a bag of stuffed animals my dad had gotten a while back, and we were never going to use them. On seeing these, a brilliant idea popped into his head. He thought that we should blow these darling creatures up. Unlike most young girls, I reacted with elation. I loved the idea. We stuffed bears, dogs, and bunnies with explosives. Stuffing flew everywhere. On one specific occasion, a stuffed bunnies' head blew clean off! The body and the head were both intact, but they were separated. Whereas most nine- or ten-year-old girls might be horrified and scared, I was filled with a sort of sick joy at the sight of a bunny head landing on the ground, five feet away from the body.

More important than our escapades was the bonding that took place during those times. Those days of colorful explosions and bunny decapitations bear fond memories for me. They were days of fun, joy, and exploration. A pivotal part in all of these memories is played by my dad. He was the one who taught me how to light a firework and never turn my back. He was the one who sparked the interest in the first place. I'm not sure if I would've loved fireworks so much if my dad weren't the one doing them with me because it just wouldn't be the same. I am not saying that this particular bonding activity is perfect for every family, but it is a pivotal part in me and my dad's relationship. We have created many fond memories by blowing stuff up. The love for fireworks is something most human beings share, and by letting your child light one occasionally, you show them that you trust them. I am not saying to let your six-year-old kid light a mortar; that is never a good idea, but find something that you and your children can do together to bond. Create some sort of tradition that you all can enjoy. I would recommend lighting fireworks every Fourth of July, but I understand if that isn't for you.

21

Stoopid

There is an unfortunate side effect to encouraging your children to dream big. Other people will doubt your child's dream because it isn't theirs. Rightfully so. I couldn't possibly achieve someone else's dream. I have my own God-given dreams and things I hope for. Still, people feel it necessary to thrust their own beliefs and opinions upon us as veiled advice. Honestly, most people probably believe that they are helping when they make hurtful comments, which hurt a person deeply enough to push them to shelf their dreams, but they aren't. So today, on a playground near you, some youngster has said something to another child that has caused them to feel hurt and unloved. Maybe it was your child who was hurt.

The protective instinct of a parent is a tough one to overcome. Kids are mean! They do things to hurt other kids just because they can. They say things to our kids that are meant to demoralize, humiliate, and crush. They do it because of their own insecurities, but my child doesn't realize that unless I teach them that truth.

Still, when your child comes home from a day at school, and you hear that someone made fun of them or bullied him/her in some way, the natural desire is to call that kid's mom and dad and have a showdown on the playground at high noon. We want to protect them from the hurt that they will undoubtedly face. We want to take up arms and fight the battle for them, but that makes us no better. What we need to do is disarm the attacker by taking away the victim mentality that completely fills our society.

If our kids don't learn how to fight their own battles, what will they do on that fateful day when you are no longer around to fight the fight for them? Teach your children how they should respond in a situation, and they'll respond that way. Teach them to find their confidence in themselves and who God created them to be, not in the opinions of others, and you've taken away a significant amount of ammunition right there. They don't need to take to physical fighting or name-calling, lowering themselves to the level of the aggressor; they need to know who they are isn't built upon the insignificant opinion of individuals who are so insecure their only relief is to hurt others. When the weapons of the attacker are taken away, they will be left with one of two options; either escalate the encounter (which most won't) or leave with a slightly deflated ego.

I've taught both of our girls to be who they are and be proud of it. Honestly, my girls are a little weird when compared to the rest of the kids in their schools. They stand out, not because of poor behavior, but due to a confidence that others find a little irritating. Society would say it isn't normal to not be moved by the opinions of our peers; and when society is confronted with something that proves otherwise, it retaliates.

Both of my daughters have been bullied, called names, even shoved. I get a little angry when I hear about their encounters, but what good will it due me to beat up the kid's dad? I'm just exacerbating the problem. Those moments have become teaching times for us. Sometimes the words hurt, but if we are confident in who we are, they can't defeat us.

I honestly feel compassion for those who would hurt others just to make themselves feel better. I want them to see who they could be if someone who believed in them came alongside them and encouraged them to rise above their own hurt. It's important to encourage our kids to build people up on a regular basis. It's so easy to tear someone down, but it's so destructive. It's harder, but far better, to encourage people to see what they could be if they forgave the wrongs committed against them and accepted themselves for who they truly are.

It's very important that we forgive those who have hurt us with their actions and their words. This is crucial because bitterness can keep us from becoming what we are meant to be. Forgive even if it isn't asked for, not sanctimoniously, but completely, without expecting anything in return.

Forgiveness is the most important step in the process, and it has an uncanny ability to change those around us. It opens doors to impact the lives of the very same people who meant to hurt us. It begins the process of healing in our lives and in our self-image.

One of the most influential things we can do to encourage a positive self-image in our kids is to let them know that it's okay for someone not to like them. You can't possibly please everyone, but if that's what your kids see you trying to do, they'll think that's what we're supposed to do. Bottom line; some people just won't like you. They won't be your friend, and that's okay! Confidence in who you are will bring other friends who are more beneficial than some of the people you encounter each day.

Teach your kids that they don't have to be everyone's friend! They don't have to agree with every viewpoint that's out there, but they need to respect the individual in spite of the differences. Very few friends they have today will be their friend for life. People move, life changes; we can't be crippled by an unhealthy desire for acceptance.

I know we want people to like us and accept us for who we are. But the sooner our kids understand the idea that everyone will like them is unrealistic, the better. Just because I'm not your friend doesn't automatically make you my enemy. It's better to be yourself than to conform to the ideals of someone who won't be there for you when your moment of need arises. It's far more important that I accept myself as I am than everyone at my school accept me.

As our kids walk in that confidence, eventually the negative voices will grow quiet. My girls have both had people say things to them that hurt them, but they stayed confident anyway. They still hurt inside. Words will sting, but they had the confidence to recognize that some opinions just don't matter, at least not to them.

They are different, and that's okay. They aren't the most popular and not everyone likes them, that's okay! They stand for their beliefs, and others disagree with them. Sometimes others even mock them, that's okay! They know who they are and what they hope to be one day. People will always doubt. Someone will always have a negative opinion and be more than willing to share it. True friends are rare and love us as we are—weirdness and all!

Bria

It has been pointed out to me numerous times that I am not normal. I am perfectly okay with that because who wants to be normal. I take great pride in my weirdness, which is probably one of the reasons people point it out to me. Most of the time, the people who tell me that I am abnormal are my friends and family, who know my position on my abnormality. I have always been encouraged by my dad to just be me. He has always told me that I should be myself, no matter what anyone tells me. I took this advice to heart at an early age and decided that it did not matter what anyone else thought about me.

This was an especially easy concept in elementary school because all of my close friends seemed to be just as weird as I was. My playground posse hardly changed from first to fifth grade. People would come and go, but the core group remained the same. I remember that not long after my mom started an aerobics class, I started doing a workout class of my own at recess. I had five pretty constant students, and some people just came and went. I wasn't really thinking about it then, but occasionally my group and I would be ridiculed for our desire to remain fit. We didn't pay attention. We were having fun doing jumping jacks and running up and down the hill at the back of the playground.

However, this was not our normal playground pastime. My friends and I would, as we have now come to affectionately call it, LARP, as in live action role play. We didn't have any costumes, but we were creative. One day, the playground was a distant planet in a galaxy far away. Another day, it would be an enchanted forest that we were trying to free from a tyrannical witch. Our games would stretch, and we would fabricate stories until the whistle blew, and it was time to go inside.

Our games were not the most popular on the playground, and one day someone decided to step out and show me that they weren't. For now we will call this girl Seven, and her friend Eight. Seven was not the nicest person to my friends and me in the fourth grade. So, try to imagine my shock when she came over to play with my friends and me one day. I was immediately suspicious, but being a friendly fourth grader, I welcomed her to our group and tried to explain the game to her and her friend, Eight. I believe that day, we were playing some retelling of The Chronicles of Narnia, one of our favorites. The whole time, I could tell that something was off. Seven and Eight were mocking us. I tried to ignore it, but it was incredibly obvious to me, and it was starting to get on my nerves. I'm not entirely sure what happened, but about five minutes before the end of recess, Seven and Eight left. A few minutes later, after my friends and I had decided our story was done for the day, Seven pulled me aside and asked to talk to me. Being a friendly fourth grader, I said yes and went with her to talk on a hillside beside the basketball court. I thought she might have wanted to apologize or something. When we sat down, she said something along the lines of, "Why do you play the games you play? You aren't going to get any friends if you keep being weird." At first I didn't know how to respond. Then I looked at her and said, "I have friends."

"Yeah," she responded, "but don't you want more friends?" She also pointed out to me that my friends weren't exactly the cool kids. "I'm just trying to help you," she said.

In my mind when I recall this moment, I see from my point of view on the hill, looking down on the playground. I see my friends standing around doing something that wasn't exactly considered cool. Then I turned to Seven. "Thanks for your concern, but I would rather have friends who like me for who I really am than friends who like me for who they think I should be." She looked down, shook her head a little, said something like "Okay" or "I was just trying to help." Then she walked away. I went in the other direction.

I was heartbroken. I thought I was about to make a new friend, but it turned out my original instincts were right. I went and told my friends what had happened. I told my dad when I went home. He expressed to me that he was proud of me for standing up for myself and refusing to change because someone else said I should. Still, I wasn't happy. For a long time, that girl and her friend became my nemesis. Her friend, the girl I referred to as Eight, and I became kind of friends later. Now Seven and I get along and can have conversations, and I would like to get to know her better. We like a lot of the same things and have moved on. I don't even know if she remembers the day that she tried to make me change. It's okay if she doesn't because I have forgiven her.

It's a hard process; forgiveness, especially when the person being forgiven doesn't even seem to regret what they did. However, my parents have always taught me to forgive and forget. I have forgiven that girl even if I haven't forgotten. I hold on to that memory to remind me that I should always hold on to who I am, and that I have people who will come alongside me even when I am not considered to be the coolest person.

22

A Dream for Every Dreamer

I have always encouraged my girls to dream big. I don't want them to be limited by what they see now; I want them to go beyond their wildest imaginings. Encouraging them to dream is great. How can I help them succeed in achieving their dream?

I think, for most adults, we lose the spirit of the dreamer through the trials of life. We become overwhelmed with the mundane, day-to-day tasks and lose sight of our own dreams. We set them aside because it feels like the responsible thing to do. We have families now, we can't afford to be chasing after those silly dreams. Deep down inside though, there is part of us that longs for the dreamer to resurrect some of the passion we once had. But fear of ridicule or failure keeps us from ever daring to dream again. Oh, we might have small dreams and minibursts of passion, but the grand dreams that drove us to lay out under the stars for hours imagining the possibilities are gone.

We tell ourselves things like "It wasn't meant to be" or "I tried" knowing that we didn't really give it all we had inside. Somewhere along the way, someone came against the dream, and their disbelief caused a sliver of doubt to form that we just couldn't overcome. We begin to develop regrets and wonder what might have been. The feeling of discontent leads us to try and temper our children's dreams so that they don't experience similar disappointment in their own lives.

It makes sense. We are just trying to keep them from experiencing the same pains we encountered, but the problem is we unintentionally stifle their achievements. We want them to focus on something practical, something they might actually accomplish, but there is no limit to what we can accomplish as individuals if we are determined and willing to pay the cost.

Man walked on the moon because someone along the way had the dream of reaching the stars. They surrounded themselves with people who told them they could do it if they worked hard and didn't view failure as the end. They stuck to that dream and eventually achieved something that for thousands of years was thought unattainable. I'm sure that there were detractors and doubters in their path as well, but somewhere along the way, those dreamers were encouraged to believe in their dream regardless of what others might think. Their passion and belief outweighed the doubt of those who couldn't possibly have achieved what the dreamer set out to do!

If you're going to dream, dream big! Don't limit what you or your child can accomplish together! How great would it be to show your child that they can achieve anything they set their mind to because they saw you pick up that dream you've been hiding in the corner, dust it off, and pursue it to success? What would that say to your child, and how much easier would it be to help carry the banner for their own dreams?

Be the catalyst that propels your kids forward, not the anchor that holds them back. We have no idea what our encouragement can do for someone, and what that moment of belief can push someone to accomplish! In the end, it doesn't matter if they fall down. Failure is ultimately an opportunity to try a new approach to achieve a desired result. We have a very poor perception of failure in our society. It's far easier to never take a risk than to try and fail. But what successes come without risk? Dreams are never realized in the dreaming, it's the doing that takes us to the place where dreams are achieved. All too often, the fear of disappointment because we fell short of the goal stops us from achieving more than we could have ever hoped.

So we offer our kids advice from the position that we are trying to help them. After all, disappointment is so discouraging. We think to ourselves, I don't think I can bear to see them go through that. It's all tainted by our own dreams that were never reached, and the discouragement that leads to regrets over what we might have been able to do if life hadn't gotten in the way.

Rather than dwell on what you haven't done, think about what you have in front of you. Encourage your children to be anything they could ever dream of being. Don't give in to that part of yourself that wants to be the voice of reason. Reason is the deathblow of dreams. There are always going to be reasons why we can't do things. Look for the reason that something should be done and hold onto that idea. Be your child's biggest cheerleader, not so that you can take the glory for their accomplishments, but so that one day, you can wholeheartedly say that you always believed they could accomplish anything they set their mind to. Tell them how proud you are and be there to support them in defeat and lift them up in victory. Believe in their dreams and remember what it was like to have a dream of your own. Pick it up and dust it off. You might just accomplish it still if you have the courage to believe.

Bria

My dad has always been there for me. I would not be halfway to where I am today without him. He has always told me that I can do anything and tried to encourage and support me in everything I do. He has sat through countless school plays, chorus concerts, talent shows, and random little plays or concerts my sister and I have done at our house to support me.

Whenever I am doing anything that involves performing in front of an audience, I catch myself (and he catches me) looking for him in the crowd because I know that he is there. Everyone needs someone to support their dreams and aspirations, and a parent or both parents, is always the first place a child or young adult looks, whether they want to admit it or not. A father should always support his children's dreams, no matter if they seem to want him to or not.

It's never too late to start supporting your child's dreams. If your child is older and acts like they don't care, that doesn't mean that is true. In most cases, it is just the opposite. Their nonchalance or even rejection toward your support is often a defense mechanism that they use to keep themselves from getting hurt, so don't stop trying. Don't give up, no matter how hopeless it seems. Eventually, that attitude will go away, and a great relationship will grow.

Another important point is that you need to acknowledge that your child's life is their own, not your second chance to experience a failed dream. Don't try to make them do something they don't want to do because it's what you want them to do. Encourage your child to follow his or her own dreams. Trust me, the outcome will be much better for both you and your child.

A father should always support his child's dreams, whether they aim to be a princess, president, astronaut, teacher, singer, or marine biologist. It doesn't matter what the dream is or how outrageous it is, it needs to be supported. Always encourage your child to follow their dreams and never tell them that they can't do it or that they are too young. When a child is small, build the strong foundation and make sure they know that you will always be there and will always support and love them, no matter what they choose to do. When a child is older, support them wholeheartedly and give them practical advice on what to do to reach their dreams if you can. Make sure they know that what is important to them is important to you. Bottom line: be there at every sporting event, concert, play, or science fair you can. Teach your child that they can do anything they set their mind to and back up that statement by supporting them in whatever they choose to do.

23

The Dragon Lady

Over our years in ministry, my wife has been given the nickname, "the Dragon Lady." It's not something that bothers her, it's actually something she has referred to herself many times over the years. It refers to that point where she has been pushed to her limit. Some of our students have had an acute sense of knowing just how far to push before she would issue her warning.

She started out innocently enough. Camping trips and youth lock-ins, retreats and amusement park trips; kids will be kids, but hotel management doesn't always understand, and my wife likes to get a good night's sleep. When the students refused to allow that, the Dragon Lady would awaken! In fact, many of our students developed an ability to sense when the Dragon Lady was about to appear, and they would warn the other students, trying to appease the monster.

It's not that my wife doesn't like to have fun. On the contrary, she does. But she likes her rest, and she respects others who want to rest so much that she occasionally transforms, kinda like the Hulk, just not green. She says her peace, and then she goes back to sleep. In fact, sometimes she isn't even aware she's transformed!

I remember one night when she had asked me to turn down the television. We lived in a small three-bedroom home with one bath. All the rooms were on top of each other, so at times, when she would go to bed before me, the TV would disturb her slumber. It wasn't her fault; the layout of the room required the TV stand to point toward the wall behind our headboard in our bedroom. She occasionally would ask me to turn the TV down so that she could sleep, and on this night, I had already done so. I would turn it down so low that I couldn't hear it sitting in front of it, so I just turned it off, went into the den, and started typing. About an hour later, she came tearing out of the bedroom and yelled, "If you don't turn that TV down."

To her surprise, the television was off. She stood in the living room perplexed because I wasn't watching TV. She had dreamed the TV was still on, and she was very confused to discover it wasn't. My wife has the best hearing when she is on the other end of the house. Sitting in front of the TV, she can't hear it most of the time, but let her head hit that pillow, and it's always too loud. I don't understand it, I just smile, nod, and turn it down.

She has had a number of incidents like that, both on youth trips and at home. We love her because it's part of her uniqueness. My girls spent so much time on youth trips with us as they were growing that they began to pick up the nickname our students had lovingly given her. They didn't mean any disrespect by it, and she encouraged it with the students. Our girls adopted it as a warning sign that they needed to straighten up before the dragon woke up.

I grew up in a family where picking on each was a love language. Naturally, my girls have inherited a similar ability to pick. But like a scab, some things and some people just shouldn't be picked at. Our girls' going back and forth at each other is one of the quickest ways for the Dragon Lady to be unleashed. There is just a point that my wife doesn't like to be crossed.

Personally, I have crossed the line a time or two, scaring her when she thought she was in the house all alone or encouraging the students or our kids to push the envelope a little bit further. Like I said, I have always had a little rebellious side. Some would call it devious. I call it adventurous, my roguish charm.

It's only natural our girls would take after me in that way. They've spent a lot of time with me! Sometimes to their detriment, my girls will get goofy, or we will get loud when their mom is in a moment that requires our absolute quiet. Sometimes she will have a paper due, other times she will be reading to unwind from a stressful day at work. Whatever the situation, we've learned to adapt. It's actually kind of funny! We all have our little quirks! As Lexy would say, "We're all a little weird in our own special way."

In reality, my wife is one of the most loving people I know. Her family's example helped me to find faith in a time in my life when I wasn't sure love could last. I thought marriages were doomed to fail. My whole perception changed when I saw what could be in her family. It helped me to realize that I could be a good husband and father. I found the determination to commit to our marriage through trials and celebrations. I wouldn't change a thing! Even though the Dragon Lady makes an appearance from time to time, it's because she wants us to be the best we can be. We all have our moments after all. She just gets a cool nickname to go with hers!

Bria

My sister and I were primarily raised by our dad. When we wanted to play with someone, Daddy was the one who was at the house to play with us. Daddy was home all day and watched movies with us and played dolls with us and taught us how to do various things. He was a constant presence that we could always count on, and we loved that.

Mama was a different story. She wasn't home all the time. She wouldn't get home until the evening, and then she was tired from her day at work. She wasn't usually around to play with us, or at least not as often as Daddy was. Mama was at work a lot of the time, and we didn't get to connect with her as much as we connected with Daddy.

I mentioned that my mom would often be tired when she got home from work. That tiredness contributed to a bit of a temper that would, and still does, come out from time to time. This part of my mom got an infamous nickname: the Dragon Lady. We—meaning my sister, my dad, anyone who really knew about her nickname, and I—often still joke about it. If my mom is around and someone does something that irritates her, we feel obliged to warn them that we are in danger of waking up "the Dragon Lady."

My mom is known for being very vocal. If she wants you to stop doing something or start doing something, she will tell you, and she isn't always very gentle about it. She can be a little bit bossy, but it is part of her nature. She wants people to be all they can be, and sometimes that desire results in some tough love.

What's weird is that I have found myself often having Dragon Lady moments. I have been called Dragon Lady Jr. before and worn the title with pride. But when I think back, I realize that when I was little, I never really wanted to be that. I didn't want to be associated with the name Dragon Lady. I was convinced that I was going to be nice all the time and never yell at anyone. However, as I have grown older, I realize that I am a lot like my mom in more ways than one, and I am thankful for that.

We still have our differences, but I often feel more connected to my mom now than I ever did before. It's not that we didn't talk before, but now I can see things in her that I didn't before. Now I'm not saying that I didn't like my mom when I was little. I loved her, and I still do, but I just didn't get to spend as much time with her as my dad, and that resulted on a slightly more strained relationship. I realize that this could be a problem for families considering the same path that my parents took. Let me assure you, it works out. There was a little bit of strain on our relationship, but we still loved each other. We still spent time together, even if it wasn't as much as my dad and I together. We made memories and connections, even if some of them do consist of the Dragon Lady coming out and spewing a bit fire here and there.

24

Taking Flight

It's a scary thought. One day soon, my children will spread their wings and fly. The question is: Have I given them the tools they need to succeed? Will they soar or tumble gracelessly out of the nest?

I'm fairly certain they are ready. They are probably more ready than I was, but I still want to be sure that I've given them every tool possible to succeed. I've seen too many young people crippled by their surroundings, not fully prepared for the world around them.

It's a delicate balance between overprotecting and underinstructing. Too much parental protection and your child becomes naïve, too little and they go hog wild.

Our kids have to be allowed to grow! Sometimes they even need a little nudge to get started, but then you have to be careful not to influence their decisions too much. It's ultimately their life and not a second opportunity for mom or dad to relive the glory of their youth. I think the hardest thing as a parent is to watch your children going through something and wanting to save them from the pain they are about to encounter but realizing it's a lesson they will have to learn on their own.

I think that's why most people at some point have the realization that though mom and dad might not have been right about everything, they were right more often than they were wrong. In fact, they might not have been wrong from their perspective because for them, the solution was the one they gave.

It all comes back to that one word, perspective. We can't make the best choices for our children as they become young adults and eventually parents themselves because we can't see the world through their eyes. It would be a whole lot easier if we could don a pair of glasses that brought the perception of others into clear focus. We could relate better and avoid so many of the disagreements that lead to delays in doing what needs to be done.

I'm not ready for so many moments in my daughter's lives that they have and are going through. That's unimportant. What is important? Are they ready to take the steps for the journey their life is taking them on? Regardless of my thinking they are or not, I have to step back and allow them to grow. At some point, I have to see beyond the little baby who held my attention so completely when they were born and try to see the wonderful young woman, mother, and wife they will one day become. Even though it's hard, I have to equip them for that day, not hold onto them in a vain attempt at keeping them my little baby forever. That's just selfish, though it is very tempting.

As much as they fight doing the right things and making wise choices, I have to continue to strive toward the day when they leave the nest, and even though they may have some rough moments, they'll fly higher than I ever dreamed. My goals for their life don't have to match their goals for their life for my parenting to be successful. My dreams for their future don't have to be their dreams! My job is to celebrate their successes with them without badgering them to the point where they no longer seek my support. It's hard to let someone grow up and become what they see without pulling in the way that you see as best for them.

Of course, parenting is a lot harder than reading this book might make it seem. The words make sense, but in the middle of situation, making the right move is hard! As nice as it would be for one book to have all the answers and give an absolute formula to raising a successful child, that would be impossible. Each child is different. Two children enter the same situation at the same moment in their respective lives, and yet the path through that moment is going to look as different as the two people going through it. Eventually, we have to stop seeing them as children and see them as people with dreams and hopes and a God-given sense of direction and calling. We need to be there by their side, with tissues in one hand and streamers in the other, ready to give advice when asked but not forcing our opinions on them.

I want my girls to achieve more than they've ever dreamed possible, and in order for that to happen, I've got to get out of the way. There will be moments when I wonder what they are thinking or why they would make such a decision, but I have to trust that if I have shown them a good example, the choices they make will lead them to the place they were meant to go.

I don't know what's scarier; being a young person about to take that first step, or being the parent who has to let go and trust that, training wheels or not, they won't fall far if they fall at all.

I can't think of a better analogy than teaching your child to ride a bike. In our minds, it's so simple! We're routing for them, cheering them on, wanting to do it for them but realizing that's not possible if we want them to experience the freedom of the wind rushing past on a warm summer's evening. We hold on for as long as we can, giving encouragement and instruction; eventually, we have to let go without influencing them to the left or the right. If we do, they might overcorrect and fall.

My dad let me go down a hill. In his mind, I had two choices, stay upright or fall; either way I'd learn what to do. I didn't think I was ready, but he was right! I rolled down the hill and came to a stop still atop my bicycle. I pleaded with him that I wasn't ready, but he knew that I was. How silly would I look now if I still wanted my dad to help me balance my bike?

The hard part as parents is to fight the urge to hold them back when they think they aren't ready. We have a desire to be needed. We want to be our children's heroes! Sometimes the most heroic thing we can do is step back and let go so that those around us can discover their own greatness. We have to overcome the fear of not being needed, and they have to trust that they can make it without us. It's the most beneficial thing we can do as parents.

I used to think it was cruel for the mother bird to push the baby bird out of the nest, but now I understand that if left to our own devices, we will lean toward inaction and comfort rather than take a risk that might not work out as we hoped. When I look at it, that's what my dad did when I screamed, "Don't let go, I'm gonna fall!" He gently pushed me to the place where I was forced to discover that I could do it on my own. For that, I'm grateful! I overcame my doubt, and now I love to ride!

Our job is to help our children along their path, not to direct them to the place we think is best for them. We can't do that if we don't let go. A gentle nudge might be required! Whether it's driving a car or choosing a home, we need to be there for support, but we should never take the wheel from them (metaphorically speaking—if they're driving toward oncoming traffic, stop them, but do it in a way that's beneficial and leads to growth!). It's hard letting them grow and seeing things that lead to pain we deem unnecessary, which we think could have been avoided, but maybe it's part of their molding process. Maybe, if we stop them from the experience, we leave them weaker for their future. Let go. Be ready to catch them, but let go!

Bria

There comes a time in every child's life when they have to stop being a child and grow up. Children have to learn to take responsibility, make decisions, and the like and leave their childhood behind. This is often a scary thought for children and their parents. Children go back and forth between wanting desperately to be out on their own and make their own money and their own rules. Parents are often worried about losing their child and whether their child is ready to face the world or not.

Children are just as worried as parents are about moving out on their own to face the big bad world alone. Sometimes they neither show it nor know it, but there is almost always a deep-seated fear of moving on without parents. It is the same kind of fear as the fear of the dark or change: the fear of the unknown. Children are used to having their parents around to constantly support them financially and morally. If there is ever a moral problem, their parents are just down the hall. When a child moves out on his or her own, they have to get out from under their parent's wings and stretch their own, and that is often terrifying.

Parents, based on what I have seen and heard, mainly are worried about their child not being ready or losing their child. Many parents don't know what life will be like without their child in the house, and that scares them. That is part of the reason why so many divorces take place after children have left the home. One or both of the parents loved the child too much, and when they were gone, the parents don't know what to do.

Another worry for parents tends to be that their child is not ready. Well, guess what parents, teens have the same fear! I should know; I am one. We are often just as worried as you are that we are not ready to face the real world without you. However, as children, we have to trust that you have prepared us well enough with the time you had. I would suggest that you as parents do the same. When the time comes to let a child go out on their own and start taking their own responsibilities, you just have to trust that you taught your child well enough to make it, and that's all there is to it. There's not much you can do at that point. If you choose to try to hold them back, they will grow to resent you, and if they need help, they definitely will not ask you for it.

So, parents, don't let go too early, but don't hold on too long. Don't try to hold onto your baby for your own sake or theirs. Trust that you have taught them well and realize that if you truly love them, you have to let them go. It can be hard, I know, but remember that it's just as hard for them as it is for you. That fear of change and the unknown is something that is not exclusive to one age group. It transcends age. Keep that in mind when it is time to let your baby step out and fly.

25

In Closing

Trust me, I get it. Being a dad isn't easy. Some discussions are just plain awkward. It's necessary though if we want our daughters to know that we love them. There will be moments of absolute joy, along with the moments of complete frustration. But take heart! The relationship you build with her today will become the foundation for her future. Your grandchildren will be raised in a home where love is the rule.

You will undoubtedly be the model for her relationships throughout her life. Establish a positive model now, and your daughter won't feel the need to chase after love because her heart will be filled with the knowledge that you love her just the way she is. She will be confident and she will take the time to find a young man who will treat her how she deserves to be treated, like a princess.

Don't discount your role in her life. She needs you from day one until the day she turns eighteen and beyond! Be there for her. Be her knight in shining armor so that one day, she can make a wise decision when the boys come calling.

Laugh, play, build memories that will last beyond your time together. Let your relationship become the heritage that follows your family for generations! Make time now, no matter how old she is, and let her know that you'll be there for her, no matter what. Listen to her hopes, encourage her dreams so that one day, she will be ready to take flight and chart her own course! Then you will be confident in knowing that you've done all you can to establish a positive example in her life.

The discomfort only lasts for a short time, but the knowledge that you love her enough to talk with her about the difficult things in life will make all the difference. It will be the foundation of who she is for her adult life. She will stand firm, knowing that she doesn't have to be anything other than who God created her to be because you showed her how awesome and wonderful she truly is. Give her the love she so desperately needs, or she'll look for it somewhere else. It's your duty as a father. Be an example of what it means to be a husband and a father. You'll have rough days, but be man enough to admit when you're wrong and correct what needs be corrected. Then you'll have a relationship that won't grow distant just because she's gotten a little older. She'll know that no matter what she's going through, you'll be there, drying her tears when she cries and cheering her on to victory every day of her life!

Bria

The father-daughter relationship is one that can be hard as a girl grows older. When a young girl reaches the teen years, it is seen as acceptable by most of America today for the dad to step back and let Mom take control. It seems to me that many dads just think they don't have much to offer their little girl when bras and boys become topics of interest. They couldn't be more wrong. Teen girls need their dads as much as they did when they were five or six.

A girl goes through several changes during her teen years, and if her dad seems to lose interest in her as the changes happen, she attributes this loss of interests to these changes. When she looks at herself in the mirror, she sees someone who is not worth her dad's attention. When she doesn't get the love and attention she needs from her dad, she turns to other things and people, like drugs and other boys. She will lower her expectations for a guy so that she can feel loved and accepted, and that is a dangerous situation.

A dad has a unique responsibility in his daughter's life. He is the example of how a young man should treat her. That is the one of the reasons why daddy-daughter dates are so important; they are an effective way to show a girl what to expect from a young man. They are not just important when a girl is little, but also when she is a teenager, possibly even more so. Teaching a girl what to expect from a young man is one of the most important responsibilities that a father has.

A father's view of his daughter is instrumental in a girl's view of herself. When she looks in the mirror, it is her father's view of her that she sees before anyone else. When it seems that her dad is losing interest in her, she immediately thinks that there is something wrong with her. This leads to poor self-image and low self-esteem. Then, issues like drugs, eating disorders, and self-harm come into play; and that is only a small piece of the list.

Don't be scared of losing your little girl. If you establish a firm foundation when she is young and build on that foundation as she grows up, there really is no reason to worry. Don't be scared to let her fly, and never be scared to give her a little push when she needs it. I understand that it may seem a lot harder to keep the relationship going strong, but it really isn't. You will have rough points, but as long as you don't stop trying, those rough points will be like tears rolling down a cheek. They are there for a moment but are easily wiped away.

A girl depends on her father for protection, guidance, and above all, love. Love is the most important thing that you can give your daughter. But not just love—unconditional love. Showing your daughter how much you love her takes time and effort. Don't back down when the teen years come because it can be slightly uncomfortable. Show her that you love her just as much now as you did before, and assure her that you will never love her any less. If you continue to show her that you love her unconditionally, you will always be Prince Charming in her eyes.

Appendix A

Basic Repairs
that Everyone Should Know

There are a few things that everyone should know! Regardless of whether you raise boys, girls, or both, make sure you take the time to teach them some simple yet valuable skills so they aren't completely helpless when it comes to making easy repairs!

Here are some links to basic skills that will help any young woman or young man make it on their own. A little knowledge can go a long way to helping them avoid sticky and risky situations!

1. How to Do Basic Car Repair
   http://www.howtodothings.com/automotive/
   how-to-do-basic-car-repair

2. Changing a Tire
   http://carrepairguide.org/Basic-Car-Repair/how%20
   to%20change%20a%20flat%20tire%20step%20by%20
   step.html

3. Fixing Air Conditioning in a Car
   http://www.ehow.com/how_2034488_fix-cars-
   conditioning.html

4. Changing Windshield Wiper Blades
   http://www.doityourself.com/stry/autorepairs

5. Checking the Windshield Wiper Reservoir
   and Filling It
   http://www.doityourself.com/stry/autorepairs

6. Checking the Oil Level and Adding Oil When Low
   http://www.doityourself.com/stry/autorepairs

7. Jump-Starting a Car
   http://autorepair.about.com/od/roadsiderepairs/ss/
   How-To-Jump-Start-Your-Car-Using-Jumper-Cables.
   htm

8. Replacing Brake Pads
   http://www.edmunds.com/how-to/how-to-change-
   your-brake-pads.html

9. Changing a Car Battery

http://www.pepboys.com/parts/batteries/diy_replacing

10. Replacing the Air Filter
http://www.wikihow.com/Change-Your-Air-Filter

11. Applying Caulk
http://home.howstuffworks.com/home-improvement/
repair/5-home-repairs-you-should-do-yourself.
htm#page=3

12. Fixing a Leaky Faucet
http://home.howstuffworks.com/home-improvement/
repair/5-home-repairs-you-should-do-yourself.
htm#page=3

13. Hanging a Painting
http://www.wikihow.com/Hang-a-Painting

Appendix B

Daddy-Daughter Date Ideas

I can't stress enough the value of dad's dating their daughters to establish a positive-relationship model in the young girl's mind. They will look to that example throughout their lives, and as they meet those young men determined to win their heart, they will use the example you set as a measure against the behavior of their suitor.

Here are some examples and a suggested start to your date as well as some blank pages to make notes and plan out a "Daddy-Daughter" that works for you and your little princess!

1. Movie night
2. State fair
3. Amusement park

4. Dinner

5. Daddy-daughter dance

6. Sports event

7. Ice cream

8. Volunteer together

9. Go shopping

10. Take a hike

11. Walk around downtown

12. Watch a movie at home on a night when everyone else is out

13. Roller/Ice skating

14. Carnival

15. Go to an arcade

16. Go to a concert

17. Roast marshmallows in the backyard

18. Do a fun run/walk

19. Bowling

20. Go to a play

Really, go all out! Nothing makes your daughter feel more loved than seeing you go the extra mile so she feels special. Dress up, bring her flowers, and open doors for her! You remember how you acted (hopefully) when you were trying to win her mother's hand. Be the same gentleman now that you want her to meet then. Exemplify the character you hope she seeks out in a young man.

A daddy-daughter date should start with you picking her up. Knock on the door, ring the bell, just make it special. Bring her flowers and tell her how pretty she looks. It may seem weird, but it's a foundation that she will turn to throughout her life.

Appendix C

Additional Resources
for Fathers and Daughters

If you would like more information about the importance of the father-daughter relationship, check out the following:

http://www.megmeekermd.com–Pediatrician, mother and best-selling author of six books, Dr. Meg Meeker is the country's leading authority on parenting, teens and children's health.

http://www.sheknows.com/parenting/articles/821928/the-importance-of-the-father-daughter-relationship

http://www.fatherhood.org—National Fatherhood
 Initiative's mission is to improve the well-being of
 children by increasing the proportion of children with
 involved, responsible, and committed fathers in their lives.

http://www.fathersforgood.org

http://www.wwu.edu/soc/bios/teachman.shtml